Kids Are A PLUS

Ray Mossholder

CREATION HOUSE

BOOKS ABOUT SPIRIT-LED LIVING

ORLANDO, FLORIDA

Copyright © 1994 by Ray Mossholder
All rights reserved
Printed in the United States of America
Library of Congress Catalog Card Number: 93-74608
International Standard Book Number: 0-88419-357-8

Creation House
Strang Communications Company
600 Rinehart Road
Lake Mary, FL 32746
(407) 333-0600
Fax (407) 869-6051

Unless otherwise noted, all Scripture quotations are from the New
American Standard Bible. Copyright © 1960, 1962, 1963, 1968, 1971,
1972, 1973, 1975, 1977 by the Lockman Foundation. Used by permission.

Scripture quotations marked AMP are from the Amplified Bible.
Old Testament copyright © 1965, 1987 by the Zondervan
Corporation. The Amplified New Testament copyright © 1954, 1958,
1987 by the Lockman Foundation. Used by permission.

Scripture quotations marked KJV are from the
King James Version of the Bible.

Scripture quotations marked NIV are from the Holy Bible,
New International Version. Copyright © 1973, 1978, 1984,
International Bible Society. Used by permission.

Scripture quotations marked Phillips are from *The New Testament
in Modern English*, Revised Edition. Copyright © 1958, 1960, 1972
by J.B. Phillips. Macmillan Publishing Co.
Used by permission.

Scripture quotations marked TLB are from The Living Bible.
Copyright © 1971. Used by permission of Tyndale House
Publishers Inc., Wheaton, IL 60189. All rights reserved.

To Brennon and Kaelyn Mossholder;
our new granddaughter, Rebecka Hinson;
Danielle Jack, Windra, Robert and Virginia Griffith;
Jonathan, Ryan and Brendon Brackin;
Taylor and Conner Tozier;
and to the kids and the kids of the kids who have
been raised in our home and become major parts
of Arlyne's and my heart.

To God be the glory for whatever you learn in this book. I felt His touch during every part of writing it — except for the passage about chewing gum!

A lifetime of love for my lady in waiting, my darlin' Arlyne. Her touch can be felt throughout this book. She has also done excellent research to help me make this book complete. As supermom and superwife she believes this will be a very important book for every reader. Thanks, honey.

Mammoth thanks to the Rev. Tim Mossholder, our son, who has also done extremely vital research for this book. The aim for every parent should be to have their kid closer to Christ than they were at each comparable age. It's thrilling when your own kid teaches you. As an expert on understanding today's youth, Tim's help has been invaluable.

Speaking of our kids, overwhelming thanks to my son-in-law Todd and daughter Elizabeth Hinson, who run the Marriage Plus office with maximum style and grace. Todd is director of operations; Beth is secretary. Their talents and skills amaze me. Elizabeth will retire this December to have a baby. Kids *are* a plus!

Abundant thanks, too, to Bill and Joyce Simmons who are steering Marriage Plus straight ahead with Jesus. Bill is director of vision, and Joyce is seminar coordinator. Both are powerfully gifted people.

Thanks also goes to each wise counselor on the Marriage Plus ministry board — president Rob Buchhelt, Max Lile, Jon Cook, Rev. Jack Duitsman and John Zachman. You are always admired and deeply appreciated.

Never-ending praise for my Creation House editor, Barbara Dycus, and her chief, Deborah Poulalion. Thanks also to Angela Kiesling and researcher Christina Williams. These ladies are a great delight. They make my writing with Creation House so much easier. So does their boss, John Mason. And his boss, Steve Strang. You're a wonderful team.

Thanks to all who help support Marriage Plus financially and with your prayers. Family and friends are the encouragement Christ uses to make life worthwhile. Ministering friends are a special blessing — Carman, Harald Bredesen, Jim and Carole Boersma, my life would be so much less complete without you.

Finally, thanks to Duane and Patricia Redic and Gary and Debra Wood of the Manassas, Virginia, Assembly of God. They bought me my new laptop computer so I could write this book with real color. God bless you for your gift. May Christ's blessings flow into your laps now too (2 Cor. 9:6-8).

Baby's feet are very small
and hardly hold him up at all.
His legs, like untied baby trees,
wobble and bend at the slightest breeze.

When my child grows up and leaves my hand
and solidly by self can stand,
may these same feet that hesitate
walk firmly down the road marked straight.

— Ray Mossholder

**I will try to walk a blameless path,
but how I need your help, especially in my
own home, where I long to act as I should.
Psalm 101:2, TLB**

RAY'S BRIEF GLOSSARY FOR
THE GRAMMATICALLY CORRECT

"Kids" = *not* baby goats in this book, but human babies, children and teenagers. Those who don't understand *that* tend to get my goat.

"Raising kids" = According to the *New Twentieth Century Unabridged Dictionary*, this phrase is grammatically correct. According to the Bible it is every parent's job. Not the government's job or the surrogate parent's job or the day care center's job, but every parent's job.

CONTENTS

Please read this before
you read this book.

S OLOMON WROTE, "OF making many books there is no end" (Eccl. 12:12, KJV). Yet he wrote three books himself! This book is about real family values — raising children and teen-agers. A lot of parents are confused about that. For example, there was the excited father who wanted to do everything just right. So as he was about to leave the hospital with his newborn son, he asked the doctor, "What time do we wake the little fellow in the morning?"

This is not another simple book on child rearing. If you are looking for a book that will tell you which end of the child to spank, this book is not for you. In fact, chapters 3 and 4 are written to inform parents just what kind of a world their kids are facing as we enter the twenty-first century. The group-think of our nation's leaders, teachers, court system and mass media must be understood or even today's Christian parents will not be successful in their parenting. Most of this book, however, contains direction for raising kids from babies to adulthood with the happiest results as they grow up.

Another word of explanation about this book: Nothing will break your heart faster or more thoroughly than a child gone bad. Parents can follow many suggestions from this book to turn even a rebel into a miracle. If you don't know the Lord and are trying to raise a kid in this present age, you need to give your life to Jesus Christ. You'll find the answer to "What must I do to be saved?" in chapter 2.

Perhaps this will help you understand the particular value of this book: In the late 1980s I wrote and taught an audiotape series for Pat Robertson and CBN called "Living by the Book." It gave Bible directions for marriage and family.

While in Virginia to do a Marriage Plus seminar a couple of months prior to the recording sessions, I stopped by the CBN office of David Gyertson (now president of Asbury College in Wilmore, Kentucky). David was upset. I asked him why.

He said, "Look at this book, Ray," and he handed me a Christian book on marriage that I had already read and enjoyed.

"I know this book, David," I replied. "It's a good book."

"How much Scripture do you actually see in that book?" he asked.

For the first time I counted the Bible verses listed in the book. There were exactly three.

"Ray," he continued, "do you realize the New Age movement could use this book as one of their texts?"

He was right. Today we tend to call books Christian just because a churchgoer wrote it or because it includes some Christian thought or a Bible verse somewhere in the text. But a few scattered Bible verses don't make anything Christian. When I handed the book back to David Gyertson, he asked me to write the first book I'd ever written, and I did: *Marriage Plus*.

Admittedly, there are at least two books right now high on the secular best-sellers' list that I have read and admired. The authors, though never mentioning Christ or the Bible, did a great job in expressing themselves. Their books (one on male/female relationships, the other on developing effective habits in life) are very worth reading. Yet if, in order to find these books, one had to weed through the plethora of best-sellers *not* worth reading — or even damaging to one's thought life — neither book, great as they are, would be worth locating.

God warns: "Unless the Lord builds the house, they labour in vain who build it" (Ps. 127:1a, KJV). You'll notice very soon that this book, like my two other books, *Marriage Plus* and *Singles Plus*, is loaded with Scripture. I refuse to write a book that teaches any other way. As Dr. Gyertson pointed out, "That's the only way anyone knows that most of what is in a book isn't simply the author's opinion, but God's Word.

The major teaching in this book has been tested and proven for thousands of years. Jesus Christ promised us, "If you abide in My Word, then truly you are My disciples; and you will know the truth, and the truth shall make you free" (John 8:31-32). If you will study the Bible right along with the Scripture references in this book, you will reach a far greater understanding of parenting.

Whenever you read a book, especially one designed to teach you something, you should know whether the author really knows his subject. Jack Hayford of the Church on the Way in Van Nuys, California, has been my family pastor for more than twenty years. With a church of many thousands I've often heard him say, "The proof of my ministry is the church I pastor." Well, my wife, Arlyne, and the kids we have raised are the proof of the Marriage Plus ministry and the things stated in this book. Our kids are all adults now. Two of the three we produced biologically are happily married. One of them is contentedly single. And Tim, Elizabeth and David are all serving Jesus Christ with their whole hearts.

We've also helped raise ten kids (mostly teenagers) from broken homes. Nearly all of them are highly successful adults now. One of them is a youth pastor. Another is married to a Christian counselor. A third led one of her high school teachers to Christ. The married ones are great Christian parents too.

In our nation today, Christians face hostile and radical elements that seem to be aiming their heaviest artillery at God's design for families. The annihilation of children through abortion; the attempt to "kidnap" the children's minds away from God and parents; the mass media's attempt at offering slime only a garbage lover would enjoy; major portions of our government pushing homosexuality and lesbianism; the public school's push of sex on kindergartners as they try to replace God with condoms; the parent trap of overworked and underpaid couples creating latchkey children and teenagers — all gang up to challenge the finest Christian parent(s).

Yet the good news is, "Greater is he that is in you, than he that is in the world" (1 John 4:4b, KJV). Hey, you can't get to the promised land of a great family if you won't go through the wilderness of the above challenges. The promised land is where winning families always end up.

I hope you like this book, or the kids who endorsed it on the back cover will be really disappointed. They — like God, Arlyne and me — believe *Kids Are a Plus*.

Happy parenting and holy hugs,
Ray Mossholder

Dear Ray:

My husband and I love your ministry. We applaud your teaching on marriage. But we are really questioning whether or not we should have any children for the following reasons:

1. The future of this world seems very frightening. War, earthquakes, disease — all the things coming before Jesus returns seem to make having any children a bad idea. Why should we bring children into such possible tragic circumstances?

2. We think there are enough people already in this overcrowded world of ours without adding any more.

3. We aren't sure that even with both our salaries we can afford a child financially.

4. I'm not sure I could raise a handicapped child. Both my husband and I want freedom from any responsibility like that.

5. Youth in today's society tend to become juvenile delinquents or join gangs. I don't want to give birth to someone who would do that.

6. My body is my own. I shouldn't have to have a child just because I'm married.

Glad to Have No Children

Behold, children are
a gift of the Lord;
the fruit of the womb
is a reward.
Psalm 127:3, KJV

ONE

KIDS ARE A PLUS

There was the mother who said,
"Junior, put on a pair of clean socks every
day." And by Friday he couldn't
get his shoes on!

THE WORLD WOULD not only be very incomplete but would come to a screeching stop without more kids. As someone has said, "A baby is God's vote that He wants the world to continue."

First the Good News

Here come the kids! All signs are that the baby bust is over. In 1992 the United States population of thirteen to nineteen years old increased by seventy thousand. According to projections from the U.S. Census Bureau, after a fifteen-year decline in kids, the baby boomers and the rapid increase of immigration will swell the ranks of young people in the next decade, increasing at twice the rate of the overall population.

As baby-boom women moved through their childbearing years, the number of births rose steadily. Births topped four million in 1989, 1990 and 1991, reaching levels not seen since the baby boom.[1]

Now the Bad News

- Only 55 percent of American adults are married.[2]

- Married couples with children represent 25.6 percent of American households, down from 44 percent in 1960.[3]

- The parents of nearly 2,750 children separate or divorce each day.[4]

- A vast National Center for Health Statistics study found that children from single-parent homes were 100 percent to 200 percent more likely than children from two-parent families to have emotional and behavioral problems and about 50 percent more likely to have learning disabilities. In the nations' hospitals, over 80 percent of adolescents admitted for psychiatric reasons come from single-parent families.[5]

- High divorce rates, changing social values, married mothers pursuing careers, cohabitation, out-of-wedlock births and even increasing life expectancy all combine to reconfigure the American family of the 1990s. An article in *Fortune* magazine stated: "Almost half of all marriages now involve at least one partner remarrying, according to the National Center for Health Statistics. Surprisingly, children with stepparents don't do any better than children in single-parent families, even though remarriage greatly improves the children's economic situation. According to the National Center for Health Statistics, they are at least as likely as children from single-parent families to have learning disabilities and emotional and behavioral problems."[6]

18

- The birthrate among unwed women soared by more than 70 percent from 1983 to 1993 — 6.3 million children; that's 27 percent of all children under the age of eighteen. In 1993 these children lived with a single parent who had never married, up from 3.7 million in 1983.[7]

- Of black children under the age of eighteen, 49.2 percent live in single-parent families, compared with 31.1 percent of Hispanic children and 19.1 percent of white children.[8]

- One quarter of all births in the U.S. are now out of wedlock, compared with 11 percent in 1970.[9]

- It should be exciting news to everyone that kids are on the increase. But since 1972 more than a million American couples have divorced each year. At the same time more than thirty-one million American babies have been aborted. While our nation fights to protect the flat-spired, three-toothed land snail and the New Mexico ridgenose rattlesnake, it is obvious it should be fighting to protect its most vital vanishing species: the American family.[10]

- If current trends continue, 55-60 percent of American children will spend some time in a single-parent family before their eighteenth birthday.[11] In 1993 eighteen million children lived with only one parent. The number has more than doubled since 1970.[12]

Fifteen percent of children under age eighteen live with step-families.[13]

- In 1990 a record 407,000 minors were placed in foster homes — up from 66 percent just since 1983...Since the mid-1980s, however, the number of foster parents has declined from 137,000 to 100,000.[14]

- About one out of four children ages ten to sixteen is physically attacked or sexually abused every year, often by other youngsters...The magnitude of the abuse is greater than that suggested by national crime and child abuse reports, says David Finkelhor of the University of New Hampshire, Durham. Finkelhor's examination included all kinds of abuse that children suffer from hitting and kicking in schoolyard brawls to assaults by adults. Corporal punishment was not included.[15]

- Every twenty-six seconds a child runs away from home. Every minute a teenager has a baby. Every day 135,000 children bring guns to school. Every year one out of four high school kids drops out.[16]

Needed: A Life Preserver

America stands at a crossroad while largely avoiding the cross. God cannot answer anyone's needs as long as they ignore Jesus Christ. This book is written on behalf of all children and teenagers in every Christian home. The future of America and our world is largely in our hands.

> You are the light of the world...Let your light shine before [mankind] in such a way that they may see your good works, and glorify your Father who is in heaven (Matt. 5:14a, 16).

You can't turn off the darkness by trying to beat it to death with a baseball bat! You simply have to turn on the light. You and your kid(s) are to be that light.

> You are the salt of the earth; but if the salt has become tasteless, how will it be made salty again? It is good for nothing any more, except to be thrown out and trampled under foot by men (Matt. 5:13).

Salt is a preservative. If there is any hope left for America's families, we are that hope. Christians have to show the way through the wilderness. Ever try a stew without salt? Ugh! In order to preserve this nation, Christ has given His people the ability and authority to be His salt through the power of the Holy Spirit.

An Assault on Salt

There has never been a time in American history when the devil has battled so hard to win the souls of our kids. An obvious, all-out attempt is being made by powerful people in high places to trample Christianity under foot. No previous generation of children or teenagers in this nation has come under such heavy bombardment from government, law, school, the mass media and even their own homes as have the kids of today. God tells us we can change this.

Finally, be strong in the Lord, and in the strength of His might. Put on the full armor of God, that you may be able to stand firm against the schemes of the devil. For our struggle is not against flesh and blood, but against the rulers, against the powers, against the world forces of this darkness, against the spiritual forces of wickedness in the heavenly places. Therefore, take up the full armor of God, that you may be able to resist in the evil day, and having done everything, to stand firm (Eph. 6:10-12).

Following God's directions, staying peaceful in spirit, believing God always, keeping your mind on Christ, knowing God's Word and constantly praying about everything are the light that will attract those who come out of the dark to receive the Christ you follow. Your kids will be the first ones attracted. But your extended family, friends and even those who seem unreachable now will "catch" what you have.

Your Family Needs Armorall!

This book is full of the ingredients that will produce the armor of God for your family. After writing *Marriage Plus* and then *Singles Plus*, this is the completion of a trilogy: *Kids Are a Plus*. And they are. For twenty-four years I've taught how to raise children and teenagers God's way as part of the Marriage Plus seminar.

Christian married couples need to raise kids sold out to Jesus Christ. The present as well as the future of the world depends on it. God's command to "be fruitful and multiply, and fill the earth and subdue it" (Gen. 1:28a) has never changed.

What God Thinks About Kids

The Bible is very clear about how God views children.

Behold, children are a gift of the Lord;
the fruit of the womb is a reward.
Like arrows in the hand of a warrior,
so are the children of one's youth.
How blessed is the man whose quiver is full of them
(Ps. 127:3-5a).

And Sarah said, "God has made laughter for me; everyone who hears will laugh with me." And she said, "Who would have said to Abraham that Sarah would nurse children? Yet I have borne him a son in his old age" (Gen. 21:6-7).

Behold, I and the children whom the Lord has given me are for signs and wonders in Israel from the Lord of hosts, who dwells on Mount Zion (Is. 8:18).

Therefore thus says the Lord, who redeemed Abraham,
   concerning the house of Jacob,
"Jacob shall not now be ashamed, nor shall his face
   now turn pale;
but when he sees his children, the work of My hands,
   in his midst,
they will sanctify My name; indeed, they will sanctify
   the Holy One of Jacob,
And will stand in awe of the God of Israel" (Is. 29:22-23).

Then some children were brought to Him so that He might lay His hands on them and pray; and the disciples rebuked them. But Jesus said, "Let the children alone, and do not hinder them from coming to Me; for the kingdom of heaven belongs to such as these" (Matt. 19:13-14).

And taking a child, He stood him in the midst of them; and taking him in His arms, He said to them, "Whoever

22

receives one child like this in My name is receiving Me; and whoever receives Me is not receiving Me, but Him who sent Me" (Mark 9:36-37).

Truly I say to you, whoever does not receive the kingdom of God like a child, shall not enter it at all (Luke 18:17).

Whenever a woman is in travail she has sorrow, because her hour has come; but when she gives birth to the child, she remembers the anguish no more, for joy that a child has been born into the world (John 16:21).

And Peter said to them, "Repent, and let each of you be baptized in the name of Jesus Christ for the forgiveness of your sins; and you shall receive the gift of the Holy Spirit. For the promise is for you and your children, and for all who are far off, as many as the Lord our God shall call to Himself" (Acts 2:38-39).

See how great a love the Father has bestowed upon us, that we should be called children of God (1 John 3:1a).

The Only Man Not Born a Kid

Those who believe carbon dating determines the real age of bones would have a lot of trouble determining Adam's actual age. He was the first man. And Adam was the only man without a belly button! He had no mother or father. Neither did Eve. They were born full grown — and failed. God immediately stopped making adults who weren't kids first.

But the greatest proof that God loves children came through His only begotten Son, Jesus Christ.

And the Word became flesh and dwelt among us, and we beheld His glory, glory as of the only begotten from the Father, full of grace and truth (John 1:14).

And Jesus increased in wisdom and stature, and in favour with God and man (Luke 2:52, KJV).

23

Get Ready for Kids

Sure, a newly married couple should wait to have children until they've really bonded. A baby demands time that, at first, the newlyweds need to give to each other. Rushing into having a family is often a big mistake. No couple is being selfish by giving each other quality and quantity time before starting a family.

Single parents can't do that. They generally bring a kid into any further marriage. So remarriage often immediately requires a very difficult blending as well as bonding of at least three people or more. Without the couple's inviting Jesus Christ to be the center of their marriage, the kids may be the first ones wanting a divorce! (Read *The Blended Family* by Tom and Adrienne Frydinger for real help. It's published by Baker Book House/Revell.)

Yet after the bonding and the blending, a Christian married couple who avoids pregnancy because kids are "too much bother" or because they're "too busy with other things" needs to realize that God says, in spite of all the fuss, "Kids are a plus."

A Few Exceptions

True, there are exceptions. Some couples may not want kids because of their own emotional or physical problems (the Lord can heal them). And God may say no because He has a special assignment for a couple. For example, missionaries going to the most dangerous spots on the globe may be wise not to have kids.

On the other hand, I've met many wives with their tubes tied and husbands with vasectomies who had used all the contraceptives known to man and — surprise! God gave them a baby! Sarah isn't the only woman in history who couldn't — and did (Heb. 11:11).

Needed: More Christian Kids

There is no "family" without kids. In this fast-paced life it is easy for a married couple without kids to begin passing each other on their way to work. They may lose total interest in home life and each other. Kids create an anchor. They become a necessary reason for being home and sharing life as a family. Without the responsibility of parenting, a husband and wife may simply drift apart because of separate interests.

Years ago, when I nearly walked out on my wife, it was my love for our kids that held me in the marriage until our family was healed by God's Word.

Nothing equals the fun and celebration a Christian family can enjoy. Laughter is very shallow when kids can't join in. What would Christmas be without them? What if there were no kids to watch grow into men or women of God?

And what would our later years be without adult kids? I've sat with grieving sixty-year-olds who look back and wonder what life was all about. They had no kids with whom to share great memories from years too quickly gone. Yes, their friends shared some moments with them. But the love their nonexistent son or daughter could have given, the happy looking back together and the "Remember whens" were forfeited. Those lost experiences can never be regained.

Pure consciences — with nothing to guard or hide — linked with wonderful memories and hearts committed to the Lord and each other are the only conditions needed for maximum relaxation and happiness after the kids graduate into adulthood. As one ninety-year-old told me on his deathbed, "Memories are all you have when you're dying. And I can't imagine how horrible this would be if I couldn't look at my kids, grandkids and great grandkids and remember all the good times. I'd hate it if I were dying alone and had no one to carry on my name.

"More than that, I'm leaving a big family that will keep right on telling other people about Jesus Christ after my tongue can't do it anymore. And to think...I'll see them all again in heaven! That *will* be heaven!"

Yes, kids can be exasperating. Someone has said, "A child's ear is a delicate instrument that can't hear a parent's shout from the next room but picks up the faintest tinkle of the ice cream truck's bell." A little boy may hand you a toad and think he's giving you a present. Or a little girl may spill ice cream on her freshly ironed dress. Sometimes kids are too noisy, talkative and bothersome. Babies sometimes need their diapers changed at the worst possible moments.

Teenage boys are the only humans who can slam a revolving door! And if Alexander Graham Bell had a daughter, he would never have had a chance to test the telephone!

But what good is all the money you can make and all the treasures you can accumulate as a married couple without children to love and be loved? Innocent, winning smiles, spontaneous hugs, honest questions, a deep desire to please Dad and Mom, a heart that can fall so deeply in love with Jesus that it never turns away — all belong to children.

And no wonder they call grandchildren *grand*children. They forever extend the celebration. Arlyne and I can't get enough of them.

One warm hug from a child or one volunteered "I love you" should be enough to convince you how marvelous children are. If you are too emotionally scarred or fearful to agree with that, let the Lord heal you. Spend lots of time in God's Word. If necessary after that, go to a Christ-centered counselor and get the help you need. Let the Holy Spirit do a miracle in your life.

Personal Responsibility: Pay Attention to God

True, the first family on earth loused everything up. (Probably because they didn't read this book!) "Cain rose up against Abel his brother and killed him" (Gen. 4:8b).

The blame game between Adam and Eve (Gen. 2:12-13) had given Cain no understanding of personal responsibility. Like his parents, Cain distanced himself from God. As Adam and Eve had responded to the devil, so did he. Like Mom and Pop, like son.

Because they had paid no real attention to God's directions, Adam and Eve might have believed kids *aren't* a plus. Cain didn't pay attention to God's directions either (Gen. 4:5). Rebellious, sinning kids become a minus. Parents who aren't following God's directions are often disappointed with their kids. And it's extremely difficult for children to live right if they've never seen their parents live right.

Prophets of Doom and Gloom

It may be true that extremely selfish or fearful people should not have children. A kid requires a big place in a parent's heart. But having a baby will stretch you. Kids will take you by the hand and pull you forward.

Some people do predict children will rebel when they reach a certain age. Such people see a mother with a new baby and say to her, "Well, enjoy it now, because soon it's going to enter the Terrible Twos, the Tragic Threes or the Fearsome Fours," or whatever other age it is when they think children rebel. Warning: Believing predictions like that can make them happen. Your positive or negative belief system *will* affect your child. The good news is: God says a child trained by and with the Bible won't rebel permanently (Prov. 22:6).

Parents Have to Work With What They Get

Please understand: All defects in a child's personality from babyhood through adulthood *aren't* the parent's fault. Friends, teachers, the mass media and other factors all play major parts in how a person thinks.

Though every kid can spit, they are not spitting images of each other. The personality of each child starts months before birth. As James Dobson puts it, "Some come out of the womb laughing. They're cuddly, warm and loveable. And they're very easy to manage. Others come out smoking a cigar and yelling about the temperature in the delivery room!"[17]

A child's walk with Christ, his own ideas, attitudes and perceptions of life will most determine his present and future. God has given every parent the honor and responsibility of shaping his or her child's ideas, attitudes and perceptions. When a parent ignores this responsibility, it leaves a terrible void in a child that only Jesus Christ can fill.

Christ and You Are a Majority

The lady who wrote the letter at the beginning of this chapter feared possible coming calamities. We do live in a world that could suddenly turn frightening. But war, earthquakes, disease and all such things have been a possibility in everyone's future ever since sin entered this world.

Missionaries sometimes face hideous conditions in far-off lands that would make comfortable Americans shiver in their shoes. Yet missionary kids often grow up to be missionaries too. When, under any circumstances, a family turns together to the Lord and follows His Word, the love, peace and guidance God brings make it clear that total commitment to Christ is worth far more than anything this world offers.

I feel sorry for missionary kids who are raised by others or are sometimes neglected while their parents go off to "save the world."

These children learn little about the great rewards that faith in Christ produces during hard times.

American Christians face added pressures today that earlier generations never faced. Yet if the people who are called by God's name will humble themselves and pray and turn from their wicked ways and seek the Lord, He will stop the calamities and heal their land (2 Chron. 7:14). Meanwhile, "God has not given us a spirit of fear, but of power and love and discipline" (2 Tim. 1:7). Christ's power, love and discipline through you will be sufficient to meet any crisis.

Expand Your Heart

As for the question, What about the surplus population? ask World Vision International or other great relief organizations, and they'll tell you that the problem with feeding people in famine-stricken nations is a matter of distribution. It is not that there isn't enough food. If Americans will give, others will live. Tragically, many countries have leaders who leave the needed food rotting on their docks.

The truth is that every living American could lie down on the ground at the same moment in Jacksonville, Florida, and nobody would have to touch or extend beyond the borders of that city. We'd still have the rest of Florida to fill, plus forty-nine other states. Our hearts, not our land, need to be expanded.

God Can Afford Children

I'm often asked, "What if I can't financially afford a child?" That's a legitimate question. The Bible says, "But if anyone does not provide for his own, and especially for those of his household, he has denied the faith, and is worse than an unbeliever" (1 Tim. 5:8).

Christian couples need to do some honest family planning to determine how many children they can provide for. Yet realize who your source is: "You shall remember the Lord your God, for it is He who is giving you the power to make wealth" (Deut. 8:18a).

One couple with four kids said, "We knew the Lord told Christian married couples to multiply and raise children for the Lord. So we simply decided, 'Less money, more kids.' We've never regretted that decision for a minute. The Lord really *is* who He says He is.

He *is* our provider" (see Matt. 6:31-33).

Many Americans believe two-career families spell success. But just the opposite may be true for your family. Shiny cars, extravagant vacations and larger TV screens don't replace happy kids and a Christ-centered family. God gave women a maternal instinct to love kids and want to take care of their own. Those who neglect their kids can easily see the terrible effect it has on their children. Divorce becomes epidemic, too, because of what outside employment of the wife often does to a marriage. What has outside employment of the wife done to your marriage — and to your kids?

Douglas Copeland, in his poetic secular novel *Life After God*, gives a stark and vivid picture of how a kid often feels when his or her parents divorce.

> And there was a story of a young child who, upon hearing that his parents were divorcing, had disappeared. A search party had been called out to comb the neighborhood and he was found, two days later, alive, having buried himself within the pink fiberglass insulation of the family's attic, trying to become a part of the house. Trying to pretend he was dead.[18]

In many cases the wife may be paying more than the total of her finances in order to be employed! The world may sadly march to this drum. But Christians who want to stay free and find the "abundant life" (John 10:10) will sharpen their pencils and add up what it costs — spiritually, emotionally and practically — for the wife to be employed. Then they'll follow God's directions (John 8:31-32). (To make this careful study, read chapter 6 of my book *Marriage Plus*. It will also give you answers to the question of whether you can afford children.)

The Single-Parent Struggle

Single parents face a unique challenge because they have no spouse either at home or employed, so both their kids and their finances suffer for it. Often, because welfare does not provide enough to give adequate care to the needs of the single-parent family, there is no alternative for the parent except to be employed far too many hours away from her (or his) kids. Thus latchkey children look for any relationship that will help fill the horrible void created by their missing parent(s). Kids from every ethnic and cultural background are joining gangs or entering into crime, violence, murder, immorality, alcohol, drugs and so forth. Our whole nation suffers when no parents are home to help guide their kids. And as for the money welfare costs — courts, jails and prisons cost far more as a result of not helping single parents and their offspring in the love of Christ.

True, there are single mothers who have kids on purpose so that they can live off welfare. But many a single parent is a victim of circumstances and honestly needs welfare money so that the family can survive. Those who live in other areas where the economy is "normal" find they often can't support their kids on what welfare pays them. Divorced parents (especially divorced mothers whose ex-husbands shirk their child-support payments) are caught in the whirlpool of this dilemma.

The idea that all single parents should be out in the work force earning their child's keep is terribly destructive to children or teenagers who need their parent to be home when they are. It is also destructive to our nation. If present trends continue, shortly after the year 2000 there will be more single adults in America than married adults above the age of twenty-one. This problem will loom far larger then.

Now is the time for the church to wake up to these tragic circumstances and provide, at the very least, Christ-centered, well-run day care at a minimum price. It is God's plan to "make a home for the lonely" (Ps. 68:6). We must help single parents cope with life by discussing their real needs with them and offering real help.

Christian couples should activate God's plan. When a Christian adult male takes a boy who has no dad to a ball game or fishing, it helps that boy recognize how wonderful being a Christian man can be. Or when a Christian woman takes a girl who is being raised by her father shopping or out to eat at a restaurant, she begins to realize how great it is to grow up as a Christian young woman.

When couples take a child or teenager out for any special event, it not only gives the single parent some needed "space," but it also provides a chance for the child to realize how good marriage can be someday for him or her. But the bottom line is that single parenting does have biblical answers and, even though the situation makes it much harder, their kids can *still* be a plus.

(Be sure to read my book *Singles Plus* if you are a single parent.)

Overcome Your Handicap

The woman in the letter expressed a desire to stay free of the responsibility of raising a handicapped child. God will most likely keep her free from that. He has promised never to give anyone a trial in life that He and they can't handle together (1 Cor. 10:13). Yet God knows you better than you know yourself. God knows what you can handle. You may not be ready for such a child today — but today you don't have one. If you ever do, God can give you overcoming grace.

Douglas Lathrop of Northridge, California, wrote this strong letter in answer to those who favor eliminating handicapped people through abortion or euthanasia:

I was born with a disability. As a child I spent a lot of time in severe pain. Today I use a wheelchair and lead an active and fulfilling life. To those who argue so vehemently for the "right" to end that life, I have one question: Are you truly concerned about my human dignity, or does my existence simply make you so uncomfortable that you would rather I disappear? To me "right to die" sounds more like society's "right" to kill me.[19]

It's a shame that more than thirty-one million babies couldn't have written that same letter from inside their mothers who aborted them!

On September 23, 1994, a deeply moving full-page ad appeared in *USA Today*, sponsored by the Economic Development Partnership of Alabama. The ad was in tribute to the deaf and very beautiful and talented Miss Alabama, Heather Whitestone, who had just won the title of Miss America 1995. The ad read: "Her doctors told her she would never go beyond the third grade. Obviously, she wasn't listening. Heather Whitestone has the ability to hear all right. It's just that through her disability she chooses to listen to a different voice than most of us. She doesn't hear those voices that tell us we're not good enough, or smart enough, or brave enough to pursue our dreams. Or in Heather's case, the ones that told her being deaf would keep her from accomplishing any real goals or even living a normal life. But, Heather, you should hear what they're saying now!"

Most other handicapped people haven't listened to the doom-sayers either. Helen Keller, Beethoven, Ray Charles, a one-armed major league baseball pitcher, many Olympic stars who were handicapped as children, a deaf Academy Award-winning actress — all prove the biggest handicap may simply be the one you have in thinking you could never raise a handicapped child.

Your Body Doesn't Belong to You

The final statement in the letter that opens this chapter asserts, "My body is my own." The writer is wrong. If Jesus Christ is our Lord, we are not our own, for we have been bought with a price. "Therefore glorify God in your body" (1 Cor. 6:19b-20).

If you are married, your body also belongs to your spouse (1 Cor. 7:4). The philosophy that tells a woman that abortion is OK because it is *her* body and her husband has no right to make this decision with her is an anti-Christ, antibiblical philosophy (see 1 John 2:18; 1 Cor. 7:4).

Childless Couples Can Still Have Children

I have counseled many married couples who have tried repeatedly to have a baby but for some reason can't. They, like me, cannot figure out how any married couple could wish to remain childless unless God had somehow personally told that couple not to have children. Miscarrying seems like a miscarriage of God's justice. Stillborns and babies who die of crib death or for any other reason cause questions only God can answer. Jack Hayford's powerful book *I'll Hold You in Heaven* (Regal Books) is vital for grieving parents at tragic times like these.

Adoption is often the winning answer for childless couples. If you can't get "customized" children, try "ready-made" kids. Ray and Rebecca Larson's book *When the Womb Is Empty* (Whitaker House) is written to help parents adopt. If you can't find a child in your color, try another color. Get a life!

The Bible Tames the Toughest

As for the question "What about juvenile delinquency and gang warfare?" kids are like airplanes — we usually only hear about the

32

ones who crash. When a gang member comes to Christ, he becomes a new person (2 Cor. 5:17).

If you have a rebel in your house now, here are some vital questions for you to ponder:

1. How much do you as a parent live the Christian life in front of your rebel?

2. How much do you as a parent live the love and ways of God in front of your spouse? (If you are separated or divorced, have you worked to keep from destroying that spouse in your child's mind? See Heb. 12:15.)

3. How sure is your kid of your love for him (or her)?

4. Do they know you love them enough to discipline them when it is required? (See Heb. 12:5-11.)

5. How much of the Bible have you made sure they understand?

6. How sure have you been that they are in a Christ-centered, Bible-believing church that is ministering life to them?

The answer to the above six questions will greatly determine even a rebel's future.

One of Our Favorite Sons

Arlyne and I have raised three of our own kids, who all love and serve Jesus Christ as adults. We've also been part of raising ten kids from broken homes. One of our most precious spiritual sons is Larry Jack.

Larry was sixteen when he came to live with us. Just before coming, he had been facing nine years of youth authority and prison. He had been breaking into homes and stealing expensive items. He had also stolen a huge truck and lost it over the side of a mountain. Arrested, he was in juvenile hall awaiting sentencing. But his sister, Diane, smuggled a Bible into his cell. It was *Good News for Modern Man.* Thank God that it was that version; it is written in fifth-grade English. He would not have been able to read a more complicated version.

Larry read that Bible and fell on his knees in his cell. Through his tears he asked Jesus Christ to forgive his sins and to become his Lord.

A judge who was known to be tough on kids was supposed to sentence Larry. But the day of his court appearance that judge got sick, and a "softer" judge took his place. Instead of going to youth authority, Larry was remanded into his sister and brother-in-law's custody.

Subsequently, we invited the three of them to move into our home. Later, when Larry's sister and brother-in-law moved on, God led us to keep Larry with us. After high school Larry became my traveling assistant for three and a half years with Marriage Plus.

Today Larry Jack has been happily married for six years. He and his wife, Renee, have just given us a magnificent spiritual granddaughter, Danielle, and Larry is a youth pastor in San Mateo, California.

If you have a rebel at your house, no matter what age nor how rebellious he or she has been, be comforted by the knowledge that when a person honestly receives Jesus Christ as Lord, "old things [habits, ways, lifestyles] pass away; all things become new" (2 Cor. 5:17b, AMP).

Making Jesus Lord means getting into the Bible and getting the Bible into us. Lordship only happens in someone when the Word of God becomes the road map for living. Larry needed it to grow into the man of God he is today. He still needs it daily (2 Tim. 2:15). So does your son or daughter. So do I. So do you.

You as the parent are the key, along with those Christians who will lovingly partner with you to activate God's Word into your son or daughter's life.

We may not be able to reach every child or teenager with the Bible, but if you are a parent, or care about kids, please read this book carefully. Every expectant mother is pregnant with powerfully positive possibilities. So is every parent. Just remember: Kids *are* a plus.

**Our kids are living messages we send
into a future where we cannot go.**

— Rev. Kevin Gerald

Dear Ray:

As a wife and mother, I grieve because I'm the only one in my family who knows Christ. I was saved after my husband and I were married for two years. My kids are fourteen and ten. My husband has refused to go to church with me, but, Ray, he's coming to your next Renewal of Love Conference at CBN. I know that's a miracle, but I'm scared. What chance do you think I have of seeing my husband saved? Even then, what chance do I have of seeing my two lost children saved in a world like this?

Praying Hard

And they said,
"Believe in the Lord Jesus,
and you shall be saved, you
and your whole household."
Acts 16:31

TWO

GOD WANTS TO SAVE YOUR WHOLE FAMILY

One reason so many kids are
out on the streets every night is
because they are afraid
to stay home alone!

I F YOU HAVEN'T thought your spouse or your kids were a plus until now, don't blame yourself. The group-think of our nation is anti-marriage, anti-kid. And kids *do* have the capability of being cantankerous, obnoxious and stubborn. Come to think of it — adult men and women, including spouses, have that same capability!

We're about to learn some very sad facts about America and its pattern of thinking today, which is having, or will have, a profound effect on your kids. That effect can swallow them. Or it can wake them up to the greatest adventure possible — living the Christian life, a life Jesus Christ described as being "the abundant life" (John 10:10b).

Anyone who interprets this chapter and the one that follows as being messages of gloom and doom doesn't know the Bible. First, there *are* answers for anything occurring now. Each person trapped in the hellishness of his circumstances can be lifted out of the pit by the One who came to do that for us all, Jesus Christ.

> Therefore also God highly exalted Him and bestowed on Him the name which is above every name, that at the name of Jesus every knee should bow, of those who are in heaven, and on earth, and under the earth, and that every tongue shall confess that Jesus Christ is Lord, to the glory of God the Father (Phil. 2:9-11).

Christ wants to save your whole family. The Bible contains the directions for real liberation. If you'll use the Bible as the road map for yourself and your family, you'll find a way out of the wilderness, no matter how thick the jungle has grown around you. With national repentance our nation could still do that too.

As you read this book, you will find resources that will help you overcome any current hassles in your home.

We are living in a prophetic time called "the last days." I believe Peter, James and John are looking down from heaven and saying, "Wow! If only we could have been ministering on earth in *these* days!"

America the Beautiful?

Let's get rid of two myths:

- Myth 1: Kids are just as they used to be. We're just hearing a lot more about what they're doing these days because of the news media.

- Myth 2: The nation is better today than it has ever been.

Both of these myths are debunked by the facts written in an article titled "The Most Dangerous Criminals in America Are Also the Youngest" by Isabel Wilkerson, a reporter for the *New York Times*. Here are some major statements from the article:

The country is facing a crisis of violence among young people unlike any before...Arrests of people under 18 for violent crime rose 47 percent from 1988 to 1992....

The rise in violence among the young crosses racial, class and geographic boundaries. From 1982 to 1992, F.B.I. statistics show, the rate of arrests for violent crimes rose twice as fast among young whites as among young blacks. Still, young blacks were arrested at five times the rate of young whites for violent crimes....

One in six arrests for murder, rape, robbery or assault is of a suspect under 18...and slayings by these teenagers have risen 124 percent from 1986 to 1991....

Young people committed twice as many assaults without a weapon in 1992 as in 1982, 143,368 to 73,987....

The violence has had a profound effect on what it means to be a child. In some Chicago elementary schools, children play during recess with police patrol cars standing by to keep order. Some high schools in Iowa have full-time probation officers in their buildings to keep a watch on the parolees.

Dogs trained to sniff out drugs and guns are brought in to search students at random in Blue Ridge, Ariz., and Savannah, Ga., and Emery, Utah, and to check lockers at night in Huber Heights, Ohio...Metal detectors are used at all student activities in Thornton Township, Ill. Some schools have simply removed all lockers so teenagers will not have a place to store weapons.

Judge James E. Lacey of Wayne County Juvenile Court in Detroit [says], "The problem is of such magnitude...It's vast. It's mindboggling. You see the failure of the schools. You see the failure of the parents. You see the violence on the streets. You see the guns. You see the drugs.

"The children are being robbed of their childhood. They are afraid of going to school and getting shot. They're worried about day-to-day survival instead of enjoying football and the honors society and the debating club and the theater."[1]

Isabel Wilkerson's article also included this quote from Los Angeles district attorney Gil Garcetti:

> It is incredible — the ability of the very young to commit the most horrendous crimes imaginable and not have a second thought about it. This was unthinkable twenty years ago.[2]

The district attorney is right. But thirty-one years before he spoke these words, the Bible had just been removed from our public schools. Before its removal, many young people had learned about God — even if only in a limited way — in classes where the Bible had been shared. Even though they didn't know Christ, they were impressed by the relevancy of the Ten Commandments and by the standard the Bible sets for living.

Parents who had also been trained up with the Bible in their schools as part of basic learning usually reinforced its standard, too, through morals, ethics and discipline in their work and marriage. They believed basic teachings in the Bible, even though they didn't know its Author.

Yes, many of our nation's families had severe problems. People did divorce. Kids did rob or kill. But a comparison of the epidemic of crime, violence, immorality and murder among young people today with these same activities thirty years ago (just after the removal of the Bible and prayer) is like comparing the Pacific Ocean with a puddle in your backyard.

The Earth Has a Terminal Illness

Revelation 21:1 tells us the earth is suffering from a terminal illness. Again, no gloom and doom pervade this diagnosis — just the absolute promise for every Christian that the best is yet to come!

If I had a terminal illness and knew I had only a few days, months or years to live, obviously I would need to take stock of my life. It would be a vital time for being sure I had done all the things I'd really wanted to do, shared with family and friends all I'd wanted to share and, above all, to be as certain as possible about where I would be going once I died. My future would be far more important than my past.

These realizations would help shape my decisions. For example, when I couldn't get my money transferred into traveler's checks for either heaven or hell, I'd realize money wasn't the most important thing in my life. At the end I'd have to leave home without my American Express card!

Furthermore, the work I'd done solely for the purpose of earning money that would soon be useless to me in eternity would make me say with Solomon, "I hated all the fruit of my labor for which I have labored under the sun, for I must leave it to the man who will come after me" (Eccl. 2:18). It reminds me of the rich man on his deathbed who told me, "I hate my ex-wife and her kids. They aren't here to even say good-bye. But they'll be in like vultures the moment I'm dead. I wish I'd never worked a day in my life."

The Bible, prayer, serving Jesus Christ with a clean and happy heart, living with my family and friends, church and avoiding sin like the plague would all take on greater meaning than they ever had before.

The only things I would regret would be sins that made me less than I should have been, words and actions that hurt others, and whatever time I'd really wasted.

As a Christian, the bottom line that I would be feeling is: Only what I've done for Christ will last.

Consider the God of the Bible

Consider the *love* of our landlord: "The earth also is Thine; the world and all it contains. Thou hast founded them" (Ps. 89:11). God could simply evict us at any time. Instead He's given us free use of all He's created and has simply asked us to take good care of it (Gen. 1:28).

Consider the *power* of our landlord: "The worlds were prepared by the Word of God" (Heb. 11:3). That's why whenever we move away from the Word of God, our world begins to fall apart.

God could simply slap our globe one time, and the lights would go out forever. If He had put the earth a tad bit closer to the sun, or put it just a bit farther away, it would have been either frozen or scorched. So would we! Instead He wakes the sun up every morning and puts it to bed every night. You can set your clock by His perfect timing.

Consider the *authority* of our landlord: "For in Him all things were created, both in the heavens and on earth, visible and invisible, whether thrones or dominions or rulers or authorities — all things have been created through Him and for Him and He is before all things, and in Him all things hold together" (Col. 1:16-17). That's why whenever we try to move away from Christ, *we* begin to fall apart.

He who put spectacular colors in His creation, marvelous tastes in food, vibrant sounds in music as well as all of life and His love in those who follow Him has our best in mind at all times (Rom. 8:28). He is worthy to be heard, worshipped and obeyed above all others.

Even when presidents, kings or national leaders seek to remove God's power, His ultimate authority and love remain. After all, He appointed these people in the first place (Rom. 13:1). And He orders all people under the rulership of His appointed authorities to obey the laws set by these humans (Rom. 13:2).

Only when God's laws are violated by man's laws does God tell His people to continue following Him, not man (Matt. 28:18-20; Acts 4:19-20, 5:27-29; 1 Pet. 2:20). He doesn't tell us this because He's a troublemaker but because He is right and they are wrong, and we would be destroyed by going the wrong way. God knows that "the wages of sin is death" (Rom. 6:23a). He wants every person to avoid sinning so that they can have the "abundant life" Christ came to give them (John 10:10).

Parents who really want the best future for their kids must not give unbiblical guidance. But the parent who says, "I really messed up when I was your age, so I better shut up entirely about what you should do," is just as wrong. Two wrongs *don't* make a right. Your kids shouldn't have to experience any tragic mistakes you made because you stay mute about the quicksand of wrong choices.

You and your kids need to keep in mind always that it is foolish to try to break the law of gravity. Those who do it always find the law of gravity breaking them. That's because God's laws (rules, principles, ways) physically and spiritually hold the world together. Personal "worlds" fall apart, too, when God's laws are broken.

Thousands Saved

The woman who wrote the letter that begins this chapter saw her husband saved in the CBN Renewal of Love Conference (Marriage Plus seminar) that they attended at the Founders' Inn in Virginia Beach two years ago.

Their children were saved shortly after she and her husband returned home.

Many people have attended the Renewal of Love, Together in Love and Marriage Plus seminars I have conducted throughout America and the world. Thousands of divorces have been cancelled as a result of these seminars, and many thousands of people have come to Christ. Most of the people saved are husbands and wives who are amazed to find themselves praying during the seminar to be born again. They never expected it to happen. Nor did their spouses — in spite of all their prayers. But no one ever has to arm wrestle God for the salvation of family or friends. When Christ went to the cross, He was dying to save you and your family (John 3:16).

God Wants to Save Your Whole Family

The above statement is so true that Paul and Silas declared to the Philippian jailer: "Believe in the Lord Jesus, and you shall be saved, *you and your household*" (Acts 16:31, italics added). Can this promise be taken literally?

> And they spoke the word of the Lord to him together with all who were in his house...and immediately he was baptized, he and all his household (Acts 16:32-33b).

How could Paul and Silas be so sure that God would save the jailer's whole family if the jailer would simply "believe in the Lord Jesus"? Because they knew God is always eager to do it that way.

> By faith Noah, being warned by God about things not yet seen, in reverence prepared an ark *for the salvation of his household* (Heb. 11:7a, italics added).
> On the very same day Noah and Shem and Ham and

43

Japheth, the sons of Noah, and Noah's wife and the three wives of his sons with them, entered the ark (Gen. 7:13).

God's miracle provisions for His people at the Passover in Egypt didn't require the slaying of a lamb for each person but "a lamb *for each household*" (Ex. 12:3, italics added).

Joshua spared Rahab and "her father's household" when the Lord destroyed the city of Jericho (Josh. 6:25).

Joshua trusted God so strongly that he was able to lead the Israelites into the promised land. He also trusted God so strongly he could say with absolute confidence:

As for me and my house, we will serve the Lord (Josh. 24:15b).

The ark of the covenant had such an anointing from God that when it rested for three months "in the house of Obededom, the Gittite,"

the Lord blessed Obededom, *and all his household* (2 Sam. 6:11b, italics added).

When Zaccheus repented, salvation came to him and his household (Luke 19:9).

No greater surprise could have come to Jewish Peter than to discover that God would save Gentiles. He had to see that fact written in the sky three times (Acts 10:11-16). Soon after that he followed three men to Caesarea and into the home of an Italian named Cornelius. As Peter preached, members of the whole household of Cornelius received the Lord, were empowered by the Holy Spirit and were then baptized in water (Acts 10:25-48).

After Lydia was converted by Paul's preaching, she "and her household" were baptized (Acts 16:15).

A synagogue leader named Crispus heard Paul preach and suddenly "believed in the Lord *with all his household*" (Acts 18:8a, italics added).

Nothing on earth is as wonderful as a Christian marriage. With your family, join these households in proclaiming, "As for me and my house, we will serve the Lord!"

Getting God's Attention in Your Home If You're Married to an Unbeliever

Over and over again I have seen a miracle happen in Christian homes. That miracle is described in 1 Corinthians 7:14:

For the unbelieving husband is sanctified through his wife, and the unbelieving wife is sanctified through her believing husband; for otherwise your children are unclean, but now they are holy.

God says mental and spiritual mind pollution is the high cost a child pays for living in a home with unbelieving parents. No soap will take care of that. Unclean, muddied thoughts grow and become habits and a lifestyle as a child observes the ways, words and walk of parents who don't believe in Jesus Christ and the Bible.

But there is still another, far more wonderful promise in 1 Corinthians 7:14. It is the promise that a husband or wife who will believe the Lord and God's Word, even when the spouse doesn't, "sanctifies" the unbelieving spouse. The word *sanctify* means "to set apart for God's special attention."

In the Old Testament people sanctified sabbaths (Neh. 13:22). The Bible tells us that God can sanctify people (1 Thess. 5:23; Heb. 13:12). People can sanctify themselves (2 Chron. 35:6; 1 Pet. 3:15). And husbands can sanctify wives (Eph. 5:26). Christians who concentrate on obeying God's Word, putting His will above their own feelings and desires, and making every effort to love an unsaved spouse will gain God's full attention and power to bind the devil. By "working together with Christ" (2 Cor. 6:1), they have the strongest opportunity to see their spouses become Christians too. *Sanctify* means "to get God's full attention."

God Saves Single Parents' Kids

God is pro-marriage. He invented marriage. But the New Testament is full of Christ-centered single adults who stayed morally pure and turned the world right side up wherever they went. (Read my book *Singles Plus*, and get excited about what God can do with singles.)

45

One of the most remarkable men of history was the early evangelist and firebrand for Jesus Christ, Timothy. Two books of the New Testament bear his name. As one would write with a pen on paper, so the apostle Paul wrote his faith in Christ on Timothy's heart. As Paul spoke, Timothy spoke. Paul often sent him where he could not go himself.

We learn something not often understood about fathering when we read 1 Corinthians 4. I have actually heard fathers say, "Don't do what I *do*. Do what I *say*." That kind of message will never be received by anyone, child or adult. Hypocrisy is the number-one reason kids turn away from parents and refuse to listen to them.

Timothy was not Paul's biological son. As Larry Jack (whom I mentioned at the end of the first chapter) is my "spiritual son," so Timothy was Paul's spiritual son (1 Tim. 1:2, 18; 2 Tim. 1:2). As Paul "fathered" Timothy in Christianity, Timothy in a sense became Paul's Christian clone. Paul actually invited Timothy (as he invites us all) to "be imitators of me" (1 Cor. 4:16b). He was saying, "Do what I *do*, as well as what I *say*."

Paul's invitation, "Follow me as an example," becomes even clearer in 1 Corinthians 11:1 where he writes, "Be imitators of me, just as I am of Christ." Paul was not urging the forming of a "Paul cult." He was highly opposed to any individuals who would form their own doctrine or develop their own following (1 Cor. 1:10-15). Rather Paul was saying, "The Christian life *can* be lived. It isn't just a grand ideal. I'm living it. Watch me. Use me as your example." Every kid needs a role model of Christlikeness. For best results, the role model should be his or her Christian dad.

A Single Mom

Timothy most likely never had a Christian dad. In fact, we know very little about his father. Acts 16:1 tells us his dad was Greek, not Jewish. It may be that Timothy's dad was never a believer and was never there for him. Not only does Paul's continual reference to the father-son relationship he had with Timothy indicate this, but in 2 Timothy 1:5 we learn it was his *mother* and *grandmother,* Lois and Eunice, who first imparted their faith in Christ to Timothy. Almost definitely Timothy was raised in a single-parent home.

I have heard people ask about single-parent children, "What chance do they have of amounting to anything? After all, they have no father to bring them up." Well, Timothy made it. In fact, he became Paul's apostolic representative to Ephesus and the regions around it. And that was just one of the items in his portfolio!

But it is important to reflect on two more things:

1. Timothy cut his teeth on the Scriptures. It was to Timothy that Paul wrote:

> You, however, continue in the things you have learned and become convinced of, knowing from whom you have learned them [his mother and grandmother]; and that from childhood you have known the sacred writings which are able to give you the wisdom that leads to salvation through faith which is in Christ Jesus (2 Tim. 3:14-15).

Timothy's mother and grandmother must have instilled God's truths in their young student. So when the apostle Paul came along to further Timothy's spiritual education, Timothy was ready to serve Christ with all his heart.

2. Timothy met Christ early in life.

Some of the greatest testimonies come from Christians who were saved in early childhood. Hardening of the arteries is a killer. So is hardening of the heart. Habits formed over years of bitterness and hate, even long after a person is saved, burp up like bad onions at times.

Once you give your life to Christ, the Christian walk is a lifetime walk that brings greater and greater deliverance from the old you. But the longer you have been a committed sinner before becoming a committed Christian, the more there is to deliver.

It is most likely that Timothy didn't have the depth of struggle with the internal conflicts Paul describes in Romans 7. His mother and grandmother brought Timothy to the Lord early. Oh, how blessed children are who are saved when they are young. Like a well-shot arrow Timothy was ready all his life to hit the target God had set for him (Ps. 127:4a).

God Saves Step-Kids and Adopted Kids

Romans 11 tells us God has not rejected His Jewish followers and that His plan is to save non-Jewish people as well. Have you ever realized that, unless you are a Jew, as a born-again Christian you are "adopted"?

> You have received a spirit of adoption as sons [and daughters] by which we cry out, "Abba! Father!" The Spirit Himself bears witness with our spirit that we are children of God (Rom. 8:15b-16).

Adoption is a very godly process. It is a heavenly plan. Born into a world of sin where the devil is god (2 Cor. 4:4), Christ ransomed you (John 3:16). And because you put your faith in Jesus Christ, God became your Father (Rom. 11:20).

Far too many Christians discover they have married a "devilish" spouse the first time around. God's plan for redeeming lost humanity has a parallel in godly marriages that take place *after* such a marriage. Kids are often transferred into this subsequent marriage. They become step-kids. Because the Bible says we are adopted into a Father-child relationship with God, it could be said *we* are God's step-kids.

Whether spiritual step-kids or God's first kids (the Jewish people who know Christ as their Messiah), we are all treated the same loving, caring way by God our Father. He loves us (Rom. 8:38-39), disciplines us (Heb. 12:5-8) and constantly watches out for our best interests (Rom. 8:28).

Thus God becomes our role model for stepparenting as well as parenting. The stepparent is to love, discipline and constantly watch out for his or her step-kid's best interests in the Lord. And the result will generally be an improved version of the Christian who raises them.

God Saves Illegitimate Kids

There was a time when I could get by with sins in my life and not feel the discipline of God. No Holy Ghost alarm bell went off in me when I sinned. That was because I didn't know God. My father was the devil.

48

> For those whom the Lord loves He disciplines, and He scourges every son [or daughter] whom He receives...But if you are without discipline, of which all have become partakers, then you are illegitimate children and not sons (Heb. 12:6,8).

I'm always concerned for people who do not find God disciplining them if they sin. I wonder where God is in their lives when that doesn't happen. An awful guilt floods me now anytime I sin. The Lord won't let me rest until I straighten out the situation. Things just go wrong when I sin. That's because I am God's son, and He disciplines me!

If you have an illegitimate child, or are illegitimate yourself, rejoice in the fact that God loves you and your child. Don't let the devil continue to throw his flaming accusations at you. Instead, receive God's love and His marvelous plan for you and your entire household. Come to Christ.

> There is therefore now *no condemnation* for those who are in Christ Jesus (Rom. 8:1, italics added).

What Must I Do to Be Saved?

I'm often asked by spouses who have unsaved husbands or wives, or parents of unsaved children, "How does one become a Christian?" The Gospel of John holds the answer:

> Truly, truly, I say to you, the person who hears My words and believes Him who sent Me has eternal life, and does not come into judgment, but has passed out of death into life (John 5:24).

If you have never asked Christ to save you, or have turned away from Him, speak this to Jesus right now: "Lord Jesus Christ, forgive my sins. I want to know You. I want to follow You. Be my Lord. I'll read Your Word. I'll do what it says. Thank You for cleansing me with Your blood, Jesus. Because of you I am now a Christian."

If you prayed that prayer in sincerity, Christ heard you. The Holy Spirit has now entered you. You are a Christian. My ministry staff and I would love to rejoice with you over your decision. Phone our Marriage Plus office right now at (206) 848-6400, and we'll pray with you, answer any questions and stay in touch with you.

You can lead any of your family or friends to Christ by having them sincerely pray this same prayer.

Now say it again and keep on saying it: "As for me and my house, we will serve the Lord."

Don't wait until you die
to be brought to church!

Dear Ray:

Help! What do I say to my teenage daughter who wants her "freedom"? She's only fourteen and thinks she's thirty! When she was younger, I thought we would always be close. Now we have a generation gap that is miles wide.

Meanwhile, I'm reading magazine articles and newspapers, watching talk shows and other programs. I'm beginning to believe that maybe I am just out of touch with the real world. Ray, could you please give me as clear a picture as possible of what may be wrong? If it's me, I want to adjust. I love the Lord, but I need His help through you. Help!

The Christian Parent of a Teenager
in a World I Don't Understand

You may as well know this too,
Timothy, that in the last days it is going to be very
difficult to be a Christian. For people will love only
themselves and their money; they will be proud
and boastful, sneering at God, disobedient to their
parents, ungrateful to them, and thoroughly bad.
They will be hardhearted and never give in to
others; they will be constant liars and trouble-
makers and will think nothing of immorality. They
will be rough and cruel, and sneer at those who try
to be good. They will betray their friends; they will
be hotheaded, puffed up with pride, and prefer
good times to worshiping God. They will go to
church, yes, but they won't really believe anything
they hear. Don't be taken in by people like that.
2 Timothy 3:1-5, TLB

THREE

THE WORLD HAS FALLEN, AND IT CAN'T GET UP!

*Blessed are the teenagers,
for they shall immediately
inherit the national debt!*

N CHAPTER 1 of this book I showed you that God has declared kids are a plus. But how can they be a plus if 2 Timothy 3 is true? Well, let's get two things straight right from the start:

1. Second Timothy 3 isn't just talking about kids. It's talking about adults too. Paul is telling us what the world will be like in the last days — *today* in America and the world.

2. Second Timothy 3 is talking about *unbelievers*. Notice Paul's description: "They will go to church, yes,

but they won't really believe anything they hear." These are lost people who don't know Christ. Some of these people are in dead churches that wouldn't know Christ if He knocked on their doors. Some are dead themselves and only considered Christian because they go to church. And many others only go to church once a year at Easter or Christmas. Any of these people may be thought of as Christians, but they are spiritually dead (Rev. 3:1).

God Bless America

I love America. No matter where I travel away from this country, there is no place like this great nation. I like displaying the American flag, the freedom of being able to say "One nation under God" when I salute it, marching in parades, voting — in short, I am very patriotic. But America didn't become America by mere chance.

I believe God chose America specifically because of the faith of our founding fathers (and mothers!). America inherited a very rich heritage from them. Since that time many wars have been fought and many brave people have died to preserve this nation. It is worth preserving. Our children's future lives here depend on it. But we cannot dare to be like old men who look back and talk about their "glory days" and forget where they are *now*. We Christians especially must be alert in this present hour if God is to continue blessing America.

Missing Bibles

A large portion of the United States government is dedicated to keeping America's children and teenagers biblically illiterate. With a stunning sweep of illogical and demonic reasoning, the United States Supreme Court ordered God to leave our public schools more than thirty years ago. The world's best-selling book — the most gifted book of literature ever written and the book that holds the key to success or failure for any nation — was removed.

The Bible was censored in a land that prides itself for *never* allowing censorship. Amazingly, prayer was also stopped by gag order in all of our public schools. The result over the past thirty years has been chaos among the young and a generation largely unaware of the truth that would set them free. In this and the next two chapters we will see what was done, who did it, and how and why they want to gain control of your child or teenager today. Then you'll learn what to do about it.

Who Would Want to Be an Adult Today?

What thinking kid would want to be an adult today? "Adults Only" usually means an offering of sleaze, booze or something else that gives you a headache. "Adult language" as a warning before a TV film usually means you are about to hear language that would make a Marine blush. In many ways "adult" just looks like the beginning of *adult*ery.

Nevertheless, kids are growing into adults. Yours are next in line. How you parent them will have a whole lot to do with whether or not they become the rebels described in 2 Timothy 3 when they grow up.

Sure, it may be a greater challenge today than in years gone by. But challenges aren't necessarily to be avoided in life. Jesus Christ promised:

> "He who overcomes, I will grant to sit down with Me on My throne, as I also overcame and sat down with My Father on His throne" (Rev. 3:21).

Overcome the challenges of parenting, and you'll be sitting with Christ in heavenly places! So let's look at the world and especially the group-think in our nation as it really is.

Doing Anything I Want to Do, No Matter What It Costs You

Humanism is the belief system that says, "There is no God. Man is what he makes himself to be." Humanists believe they know what is best for every other human because of their superior intellects.

The basic problem with humanism is that it is full of "I" trouble. It requires tremendous conceit to be a real humanist. In fact, a dedicated humanist by his own selfishness concludes (whether he verbalizes it or not) that *he* is his own god. Thus he attempts to set by force what he believes are the correct standards and laws for all mankind, no matter what anyone else believes.

One of the most dangerous human beings in this world is a humanist with power in government, court systems, the mass media or in any position to teach. As the Bible warns us:

> Since they did not see fit to acknowledge God any longer, God gave them over to a depraved mind, to do those things which are not proper, being filled with all unrighteousness, wickedness, greed, evil; full of envy, murder, strife, deceit, malice; they are gossips, slanderers, haters of God, insolent, arrogant, boastful, inventors of evil, disobedient to parents, without understanding, untrustworthy, unloving, unmerciful; and although they know the ordinance of God, that those who practice such things are worthy of death, they not only do the same, but also give hearty approval to those who practice them (Rom. 1:28-32).

Many people follow the humanists because they are in total awe of these pseudo-intellectuals. No matter how off the wall it may be, humanists can say almost anything in such a way that their followers will goose-step to the humanist's drumbeat.

That's how Adolf Hitler took control of Germany and Joseph Stalin took control of Russia. It's how dictators anywhere rule and reign. Those who don't agree with humanists are eventually destroyed by them. As with Hitler or Stalin, however, the humanists eventually lose their followers because their total depravity becomes visible to everyone, and they, or at least their philosophies, are destroyed.

It took seventy years for the Russian humanists under communism to come to their well-deserved overthrow. But the horror that the people suffered there is beyond any description. There are still many people in high places who would like to return Russia, and even Nazi Germany, to their former state.

Humanists destroy kids' minds, or abort the kids — whichever is most convenient to their humanistic selfishness.

Today America is full of humanists who ignore God and want only their "rights." They want women's rights, children's rights, animal rights, gay rights, abortion rights and so forth. And if America continues in the way it is going, it will soon be given last rites!

Are Christians Right or Wrong About Right and Wrong?

Jo Artis Donita screamed, "You guys are so unfair!" to a judge and prosecutors. She had just been sentenced to ten years in prison and denied custody of her three-year-old son. What had Donita done? She had beaten her son until he was blind, deaf and unable to walk.[1]

Question: Was Donita right? Since the boy was her child to begin with, had she done wrong?

I ask the above question because there are millions of humanists today who do not believe in right or wrong. They believe we live in a world of no absolutes. Since nothing really matters, they should be able to do anything they want to do.

The Bible Is the Book of Absolutes

In 1971 I stood in front of the Sacre Couer Church in Paris, France, the most beautiful church I've ever seen. In the evening darkness, the special lighting made the white building glisten. But when I turned away, I saw scores of street people on a grassy knoll in front of the church, beating strange rhythms on bongo drugs and obviously either stoned on drugs or drunk. Some were graphically engaged in physical passion.

This spectacular church represented God to many people in Paris, but it failed to reach these lost people. Moved by this fact, I thought out loud: "If only they knew Jesus, this wouldn't be happening."

A humanistic German philosophy professor stood next to me. He decided he'd straighten me out once and for all. "There is no truth," he hissed.

I smiled and asked, "Is *that* the truth?"

"There are no facts," he angrily responded.

"Is *that* a fact?" I asked.

Now he was furious. "There is *no right or wrong.*"

I didn't want to make him any angrier but retorted, "Well, either you're right or you're wrong about that!"

Suddenly an angry sneer crossed his face as he made the humanistic statement that ends all arguments: "There are *no absolutes.*"

I couldn't resist one last response. "Are you absolutely sure?"

Then I reminded him that if he was absolutely sure there are no absolutes, then there is an absolute — the absolute that there are no absolutes!

Immediately I talked with him about the absolute Jesus Christ and the absolute Bible.

The Bible says humans may go wrong in a number of directions but right only in one. Parents need to know what that one way is. The Bible is the book of absolutes.

A Few of God's Absolutes

Consider, for example, these absolutes:

- "The wages of sin is death" (Rom. 6:23a).

- "Flee immorality. Every other sin that a man commits is outside the body, but the immoral man sins against his own body. For you have been bought with a price; therefore glorify God in your body" (1 Cor. 6:18,20).

- "Do not be deceived: Bad company corrupts good morals" (1 Cor. 15:33).

- "And this is the message we have heard from Him and announce to you, that God is light, and in Him there is no darkness at all. If we say that we have fellowship with Him and yet walk in the darkness, we lie and do not practice the truth; but if we walk in the light as He Himself is in the light, we have fellowship with one another, and the blood of Jesus His Son cleanses us from all sin" (1 John 1:5-7).

No room for debate. No shades of gray when you teach the above truths to your kids. They *are* absolutes.

My Wife's "Unforgivable Sin"

A few years ago Arlyne was driving to the store when she came to a red light. She stopped. When the arrow pointing left turned green, she started to make her turn.

Suddenly a speeding driver racing to beat a red light plunged into the intersection and smashed into my wife's car. That driver came within inches of killing Arlyne. Her car was nearly totaled.

The other car continued all the way through the intersection, crashed into a huge post and knocked it to the ground. The driver subsequently sued Arlyne for turning left!

It took several years before the court trial began. The verdict was a typical conclusion of humanism: The man who ran his car through the red light was judged 68 percent guilty. But Arlyne was judged 32 percent guilty. Why? It's very simple: My wife had dared to turn left on a green light, and if my wife didn't exist, there would have been no accident. Therefore, since my wife did exist, she was judged 32 percent guilty!

This same kind of decision is constantly made today in America's courts. Victims' rights are set aside. Criminals are protected.

In 1993, [prison] inmates filed nearly 33,000 civil suits in federal courts — a stunning 14 percent of all federal lawsuits....In Arizona, 70 percent of all lawsuits brought against the state are by prisoners....[As a result of such lawsuits] "prison inmates have demanded and won access to pornography," says Pam Smith-Steward, a senior staff attorney for the California Department of Corrections.

One inmate who tortured and killed his own infant daughter wrote sadistic stories in exchange for pornographic photos of women being tortured. When the prison staff confiscated and destroyed the photos, he sued in federal court. California taxpayers ended up paying the prisoner conpensation....The Florida Department of Corrections has been forced to allow into state prisons virulently racist materials intended to incite hatred of whites.[2]

It's the kind of thing that happens in a world of "no absolutes." And this is the world our school system seeks to impose on our children. Once more, it is a case of the humanistic belief of no absolutes.

The Evolution Revolution

Hitler once said, "The great masses of people...will more easily fall victims to a big lie than to a small one."[3] Few theories are as unproven and full of holes, yet taught as gospel truth by their proclaimers, than the theory of human evolution. In many states it is against the law to teach creation science in public classrooms. But no matter how long it is pushed on our kids, evolution will never evolve into a fact. Yet since there are so many who believe there are no absolutes, reason becomes relative.

The single most important point these proclaimers try to make you believe is: "No single essential difference separates human beings from other animals."[4] Overlooked entirely is the fact that no giraffe or hippo, though it may have a brain, will ever ask Jesus Christ into its heart.

True, the Lord may "delight" us by returning our favorite pets to us (see Ps. 37:4), but it is *the human spirit* that separates humans from all other animals and makes him the highest form of creation God placed on earth. Genesis tells us:

> Then God said, "Let us make man in our image, according to our likeness, and let them rule over the fish of the sea, and over the birds of the sky and over the cattle and over all the earth, and over every creeping thing that creeps on the earth." And God created man in His own image, in the image of God He created him; male and female He created them (Gen. 1:26-27).

The theory of human evolution is not so insulting to you and me when we are compared to monkeys. (Most monkeys are cute!) But when our omnipotent God is compared to a monkey, the comparison is blasphemous — not to mention ridiculous.

A simple insect like the bombardier beetle proves creation, not evolution. A bombardier beetle is a ground beetle that doesn't like to be disturbed. When it is disturbed, it ejects a volatile fluid from its abdomen with a popping sound and a puff of smoke. Can you do that? Can your dog do that? No other insect, fish or animal can. Had the bombardier beetle been an evolutionistic creature of trial and error, it would have blown itself to kingdom come!

When you visit Australia, with its wombats and kangaroos found nowhere else in the world, or study the intricacies of the human eye and a myriad of other marvelously created features in mankind alone, the human evolution theory gets silly fast.

Yet if teachers can somehow convince kids that we are no more important than any other animal, then humanism will gain control of our nation.

Tragically, even some Christian churches, schools, Bible colleges, universities and seminaries have pastors or teachers who teach humanistic theory because they learned it from their university teachers and textbooks.

Follow this to its logical conclusion: If we are but the extension of a single-celled organism, comparable to a blowfly or a frog, then we should not be treated better than any other creature. Murder is to be expected and should certainly go unpunished. (After all, how many cows, fowl and fish are slaughtered annually just to feed humans?)

Humanistic thinking sees no difference between human experimentation and animal experimentation. If we can dissect a frog, why not dissect a human? This kind of thinking left no shame or stinging conscience with the doctors who "dissected" living people during "experiments" at Auschwitz or other concentration camps during World War II.

In fact, today there are many who are ready to abort the baby and save the whale!

Humanists believe sex is simply the biological impulse of Homo sapiens. Such thinking can have a permanent effect on your son or daughter. So let's test the theory of human evolution from another unproven form of evolution.

My Most Amazing Wristwatch

I have a most amazing wristwatch. How can I explain it? One day while I was minding my own business I felt a strange sensation on my left wrist. When I looked at my wrist, I saw a gold spot. Just one gold spot. But soon other spots appeared too, and within a few minutes a gold watchband hung on my wrist. I feared I might be hallucinating, but I hadn't even drunk a diet coke! Not only that, but numbers, two "sticks" and a dial appeared and formed into an instrument with which I've been able to tell the time of day or night ever since.

I am told by scientific experts that my watch is a onetime phenomenon. That somehow my watch is a single-celled organism that swam in a primordial "soup." It had climbed out of a swamp in a country thousands of miles away from America and had to cross the sea to reach my wrist. Now all of this isn't the most amazing fact about my wristwatch. Far more difficult, perhaps, for you to believe is the fact that my wristwatch had *no designer or creator!*

If you believe that story, I have a rain forest in the Sahara I'd like to sell you!

The God of the Bible *is* the designer and creator of the universe (Gen. 1:1). But can intelligent humans accept that fact? Perhaps this will help:

When Harald Bredesen interviewed Prime Minister Menachem Begin of Israel, the prime minister told him: "When I was in a communist concentration camp in Poland, my interrogator asked me, 'How can a rational person believe in God?'

" 'How can a rational person *not* believe in God?' I replied. 'Einstein believed in God!' "

Dennis Petersen teaches seminars internationally on creation versus evolution. In his powerful book *Unlocking the Mysteries of Creation,* he quotes Wernher Von Braun, who spoke about the great need for scientific honesty among scientists.

> One cannot be exposed to the law and order of the universe without concluding that there must be design and purpose behind it all...The better we understand the intricacies of the universe and all it harbors, the more reason we have found to marvel at the inherent design upon which it is based....
>
> To be forced to believe only one conclusion — that the universe happened by chance — would violate the very objectivity of science itself...What random process could produce the brains of a man or system of the human eye?...They [evolutionists] challenge science to

prove the existence of God. But must we really light a candle to see the sun?...They say they cannot visualize a Designer. Well, can a physicist visualize an electron?...What strange rationale makes some physicists accept the inconceivable electron as real, while refusing to accept the reality of a Designer on the grounds that they cannot conceive Him?...It is in scientific honesty that I endorse the presentation of alternative theories for the origin of the universe, life, and man in the science classroom. It would be an error to overlook the possibility that the universe was planned rather than happening by chance.[5]

Destructive Belief Systems

Thomas Edison said,

"There are more frauds in science than anywhere else...[Scientists] have time and again set down experiments as done by them, curious out-of-the-way experiments that they never did and upon which they founded so-called scientific truths. Try the experiment and you find the result altogether different."[6]

The Bible is not a science textbook, but it is totally scientific. Once anyone understands the world had to have a creator and His name is Jesus Christ (John 1:3; Col. 1:16), everything the Bible covers makes sense. In fact, any book whose writing was completed nearly two thousand years ago and stands up in every verse to scientific examination today *had* to be written by the mind of God. Who else would have known these things *then?*

Sin makes no logical sense: get drunk, get sick and lose control of your own mind! Take drugs; fry your brain! Have sex outside of marriage; get a venereal disease or unwanted pregnancy! All three of these sins often bring death to those who do them — or someone else dies because of their folly. "Succeed" at any sin, and your conscience will torment you — or you will live in denial — for the rest of your life.

Karl Marx was right about one thing. He said, "Religion is the opiate of the people." But the Bible doesn't offer *religion*. It gives answers that will fulfill human life (John 10:10). Major religions —

even Christianity without the reality of a transformed life through Christ — certainly don't have the answers.

Examine the thinking of another major religion today: In the Hindu rat temples of India, rats are fed trainloads of grain in the belief that it will keep the spirits of dead relatives who "inhabit" these rats from being angry — while millions of Indian people starve, many dying daily in the streets.

Fantasies Don't Deal With Consequences

Nathan McCall is a reporter for the *Washington Post*. He is also a man who spent three years in prison. In one of his articles he wrote:

> Gangsters, guns and violence have always held a fascination for Americans, and blacks like me are no different. I'll never forget the first time I went with some buddies in the early 1970s to see *The Godfather*. I was mesmerized by the movie's shootouts, retaliatory murders and the ruthless gangster code. They had a way of resolving conflict that was appealing to a teenager trying to work through the murky rites of manhood.
>
> The message I picked up was: if somebody double-crosses you, he deserves to die.... I eventually got my chance to do the Godfather thing when an older guy in the neighborhood threatened my girl. Because that dude had offended my lady and, by extension, disrespected me, I concluded: he deserved to die....
>
> I gunned him down. It was like one great fantasy, as glorious as the gangland slayings in the movie. After he collapsed, I stood over him, proud that I'd upheld the Godfather code. But later that night, as I was finger-printed and booked at a police station, the fantasy faded. That's when I shed my pseudo-gangster persona and discovered I was a silly, scared teenager who was mixed up in the head.
>
> When a policeman told my stepfather and me that the man I shot might die, I became mired in the weirdest illogic: if he died, I'd be charged with murder, yet I would have denied to the end that I was a murderer.

Why wasn't I prepared to accept the consequences of my actions? Because, on some level, I was certain that the person who shot the guy was not really me — it was some person I'd thought I'd wanted to be. I'd been fantasizing, and fantasies don't deal with consequences.[8]

The humanists of the entertainment industry and the mass media, making billions of dollars off you and your kids, will usually deny that anything they film, sing or write could possibly have a negative effect on the human mind. But could they be wrong? Big business thinks so. That's why they spend billions of dollars on television ads for one minute of air time to get your kids and you to salivate over their products. Unless somehow the public reaction is so intense that it starts to cost them money, humanism doesn't care who else gets hurt if the humanist profits from it.

Growing Up Too Fast

The letter writer at the start of this chapter lamented that her daughter was only fourteen but acted thirty. A lot of teenagers would like to believe they are more mature than they are. The rest of this book will help you help them.

Be careful what television programs, movies, magazines and books you let your (or those of your kids) eyes and mind receive. "The helmet of salvation" (Eph. 6:17) is meant to cover both your eyes and your ears (Job 31:1). Most of the mass media presents an endless parade of humanism. You and your children may be spending way more time with the world than with the Lord.

Humanism = Doing Away With Guilt

John Dewey, who has often been called the "father of modern education," was a humanistic pragmatist. He was a champion of nonconformity (life without absolutes). In his *Early Works* he wrote:

> It is quite clear that there cannot be two sets of ethical principles, or two forms of ethical theory, one for life in the school, and the other for life outside the school.[9]

But guilt can't be done away with just by wishing it was gone. Charles Manson proved that!

Humanism = Life Doesn't Matter

Another one of the early gurus of humanism was Aldous Huxley, author of *Brave New World* and many other books. Here is his honest confession and perhaps the clearest explanation ever put in print of why people become humanists. It is from Huxley's autobiographical book *Ends and Means*:

> I had motives for not wanting the world to have a meaning; consequently assumed that it had none. And was able without any difficulty to find satisfying reasons for this assumption...Those who detect no meaning in the world generally do so because, for one reason or another, it suits their books that the world should be meaningless....
>
> The philosopher who finds no meaning in this world is not concerned exclusively with a problem in pure metaphysics. He is also concerned to prove that there is no valid reason why he personally should not do as he wants to do, or why his friends should not seize political power and govern in the way that they find advantageous to themselves....
>
> For myself, as no doubt, for most of my contemporaries, the philosophy of meaninglessness was essentially an instrument of liberation. We objected to the morality because it interfered with our sexual freedom...We objected to the political and economic system because...these systems claimed that in some way they embodied the meaning (a Christian meaning they insisted) of the world.[10]

Aldous Huxley chose to be an atheist. He and his contemporaries wanted to be immoral, and the Bible and Christian thought interfered with that desire. They also resisted political and economic systems that might be considered Christian. Today many in powerful positions within our federal and state governments, the judicial system, the mass media and the school systems nationwide are "Huxleyites" or humanists. "Executive privilege" protects politicians from keeping many of the laws that govern the rest of America. It seems they get away with murder!

If there is no meaning to life, then what happens to truth? The answer came from the German philosophy professor who spoke to me in Paris: "There is no truth." This attitude is evident in television, radio, newspapers and magazines — our daily sources of news. Accuracy becomes fuzzy, checking out a story for truth becomes basically pointless, surveys show whatever the people in power want to "prove."

In fact, propaganda, false reporting and news cover-ups become a way of life. Immorality or dishonesty among political leaders is held in total secrecy unless that person or persons suddenly falls out of favor with the humanistic agenda. It is always necessary for biblical Christianity to be ridiculed and stopped as much as possible in order for the current atheistic philosophy to advance.

Education reflects the current controlling philosophy, be it communism, socialism, any other-ism or a gay society. (Sodom and Gomorrah were led by a gay society: Jude 7-8.)

People can see only so much gore, tragedy, violence or sorrow on the screen without becoming numb to it, being absorbed by it or totally ignoring it. Screenwriters make these things so realistic that reality and fiction become blurred in our minds. We have a tendency to weep for some fictional character in a movie but remain emotionless when CNN shows scenes of slaughter in far-off countries. After all, within a few moments CNN will give you the ball scores, as if they mattered equally as much. To many people they matter far more!

Closer to home, nothing proves how numb to truth America is getting than the O. J. Simpson arrest and murder trial turned into a spectacular "Murder He Wrote" by the media. Multimillions of dollars are being spent by news agencies to cover the story. Who cares that even false information is treated as gospel truth by newscasters? It's far more fun for the whole world to play armchair detective than to weep over two humans who were slain, or a football legend being totally dishonored. Obviously America no longer believes a person is innocent until proven guilty.

Aldous Huxley Said Life Doesn't Matter

It is a worthwhile question: Does life matter? If life doesn't matter we could abort any life — in or out of the womb — and it wouldn't matter. Wars could be fought for whatever could be gained from them, and who would care? The slaughter of the innocents wouldn't bother us, no matter how many millions were killed. Humanistic thinking is absolutely essential for dictators, savages and all who would seize power at whatever price.

But think again: Those of you who have been victims of incest, rape or physical abuse, or those of you who have experienced the death of someone you love, doesn't life matter? And if it doesn't matter, why were you filled with so much pain?

Yet those who inflict that pain have to believe that life doesn't matter. Or course, there is always an exception to the rule: They do believe *one* life matters — their own.

Kids need parents to expose the total depravity of humanistic thinking. They need to recognize that lying, cheating, compromise, torture and murder are the ways of life for dedicated humanists. Ask your kids, "If lying and compromise are to replace purity, an honest lifestyle and the Bible by which we as Christians are to live — who will set the new standards? Who is to determine the laws?"

Think about it: If abortion isn't murder, then why would euthanasia be murder? If two victims' lives don't really matter, and it takes three violent crimes to put someone in prison for life, why not six? or eight? If gay rights are to be funded by our government, why not fund "adulterer's rights"? At least most Americans would find adultery far more normal than homosexuality! In fact, why make laws at all?

Jesus warned us:

> "Avoid blind guides. If the blind lead the blind, they'll both fall into a ditch!" (Matt. 15:14).

As Christian parents we must take a strong offensive stand against humanism and guide our kids into the reality of a life with meaning — the transformed lifestyle of a committed Christian.

Moral Leadership Matters

It is the individual belief system of each person — and especially those in high office — that will most affect our nation's progress or bring about its spiritual defeat. God says morals matter greatly. (Read the book of Jude.)

Multitudes of laws affecting the moral persuasion of all the people, and the people's children, will be made by the sway of the leaders' personal beliefs. God tells us we need godly leadership: "Righteousness exalts a nation. But sin is a disgrace to [any] people" (Prov. 14:34).

Don't Get Bitter

See to it that no one comes short of the grace of God;
that no root of bitterness springing up causes trouble,
and by it many be defiled (Heb. 12:15).

Bitter Christians are useless Christians. They do more harm than good. Out of order themselves, they can never bring the nation back to order. In fact, it is impossible to stay mad at someone and be a Christian (Matt. 6:14-15). Hate is like acid. It destroys the container.

Yet there is a righteous, godly anger: "Be angry, and yet do not sin" (Eph. 4:26a).

Acts of hateful violence are *never* Christian. But when righteous anger motivates you to Christlike action that will stop sin, God will give you all the power needed to perform it.

What's a Christian to Do?

The way to change this present darkness in our nation must be through praying "for all who are in authority," from the president and first lady to every federal or state authority who represents you (1 Tim. 2:1-4).

Pray for them to come to Christ for their own salvation and to make righteous decisions that will bring wholeness to them personally and to our entire nation. And pray that all who claim to be Christians will return to the Bible and its Author, living the abundant, honest lifestyle God calls us to live (John 10:10a; 2 Chron.

7:14). Then Christian letters, phone calls and votes will have the power to change what needs to be changed.

Your kids deserve a future worth living. It's in your hands right now. It's time to resist the devil (Eph. 6:12-13) and realize: "Greater is He who is in you than He who is in the world" (1 John 4:4b). We can still stand firm in the future (and so will our kids) if we'll go to our knees today and follow our Lord through His Word.

**What's done to children,
they will do to society.**

— Karl Menninger

Dear Ray:

We have a high school principal living next door to us who is in the New Age movement. He laughs at us constantly because my wife and I are Christians. He says that the Bible should be burned, that it's an ancient book full of myths.

He says he's thrilled our courts are smart enough to ban it from public school classrooms because that's why the Pilgrims came to America. They wanted to keep the Bible and church from dictating to the schools and government. [He says] that Benjamin Franklin didn't just fly kites. He worked hard to create the division of church and state.

Can you help us, Ray? I don't know what to tell him. We sure don't want our kids to miss out on fun and a good education. But we believe in Jesus Christ and the Bible. We think it's right that our daughter says she'll pray if she speaks at her graduation. Are we right or wrong about wanting that?

Needing Bible Answers

But evil men and impostors will proceed
from bad to worse, deceiving and being
deceived. You, however, continue in the things
you have learned and become convinced of,
knowing from whom you have learned them;
and that from childhood you have known
the sacred writings which are able to give
you the wisdom that leads to salvation
through faith which is in Christ Jesus.
2 Timothy 3:13-15

FOUR

OUR "DANGEROUS" HOLY BIBLE

Seen on a bumper sticker:
"Read the Bible — it'll
scare the hell out of you."

THE BIBLE WARNS in Romans 12:2a (Phillips): "Don't let the world squeeze you into its mold."

Be assured: You will either follow the Bible's directions and give the same directions to your kids, or this present-day culture will squeeze you and your family into its mold. In fact, it will chew you up and spit you out one at a time. The choice is up to you. But here is God's invitation from Romans 12:1-2:

And so, dear brothers [and sisters], I plead with you to give your bodies to God. Let them be a living sacrifice, holy

— the kind He can accept. When you think of what He has done for you, is this too much to ask (TLB)? And do not be conformed to this world, but be transformed *by the renewing of your mind* (NAS, italics added). Then you will learn from your own experience how His ways will really satisfy you (TLB).

The answer to humanism, atheism, agnosticism, communism, socialism and every other Christless power that seeks to take control of man is the Bible. Once a person knows Jesus Christ as Lord, the Bible is to become "a lamp" to guide his or her feet (Ps. 119:105). Until that time every human remains in the dark.

It is a colossal understatement to say that the Bible is an amazing book. It tells us from whence we've come, what to do while we're here and where we're going. Small wonder it is the best-selling, most oft-quoted book in the world. It well deserves first place.

But there are those who don't want to face what the Author of the Bible has written. Mark Twain was very honest when he wrote: "It ain't those parts of the Bible that I can't understand that bother me. It's the parts that I do understand."[1]

Why Do Humanists Want Christianity Stopped?

I saw the outworking of the humanistic philosophy in the late 1960s when at the height of the Vietnam war I covered a riot as a radio newsman in Port Chicago, California. Two hundred university-age kids were blocking napalm trucks from coming into port. One of the people I interviewed that day was a police chief. I was startled to hear that chief say, "The reason these kids are rioting is because of the *churches* of America! They preach about sin. If the churches didn't say anything about right and wrong, no one would be concerned about napalm and what it does to humans. The churches ought to be closed down!"

In retrospect, I realize the police chief's attitude shouldn't have shocked me. His thought echoed the voice of humanism. Many powerful forces in America and the world today are totally committed to the humanistic philosophy. It is the humanists in each political party who are anti-Bible and anti-Christian. This is true even when the humanists attend church, quote the Bible and claim to be Christians.

Christian Bashing

Columnist Patrick J. Buchanan wrote:

> The grandchildren of the men and women who came here to make America "God's country" now hear their Christian faith equated with bigotry, and themselves declared unfit for participation in political life by virtue of their religious beliefs...
>
> What's the Christian bashing all about? Simple. A struggle for the soul of America is under way, a struggle to determine whose views, values, beliefs and standards will serve as a basis of law. Who will determine what is right and wrong in America...Christian conservatives are not liars and haters; rather, they are the victims of lies and the targets of hatred...They want the right to life of unborn children protected. They want the popular culture to reflect the values of patriotism, loyalty, bravery and decency it used to reflect not so long ago. They want magazines, movies, and TV shows depolluted of raw sex, violence and filthy language, just as they want rivers and beaches detoxified of raw sewage. They want the schools for which they pay taxes to teach the values in which they believe. They want kids to have the same right to pray they had. And, yes, they do want chastity taught as morally right, and traditional marriage taught as the God-ordained and natural norm. Is that so wicked and sinister an agenda?[2]

God "Legally" Kicked Out!

On June 25, 1962, a loud rumbling must have been heard under the gravestone of Thomas Jefferson. On June 17, 1963, the body of Jefferson must have rolled over in its grave! Jefferson was being falsely accused by our U.S. court system of masterminding the division of church and state. No court — Supreme or otherwise — could have substantiated this accusation from the Constitution or

Thomas Jefferson's real beliefs. Jefferson's words were lifted out of context. The First Amendment clearly denied such a division, except to clarify that the state was never to stop the church.

The First Amendment clearly reads:

> "Congress shall make no law respecting an establishment of religion, or prohibiting the free exercise thereof."

David Barton in his *America: To Pray or Not to Pray* explains:

> The sudden and dramatic restructuring of educational policies was precipitated by the Court's reinterpretation of *separation of church and state*. The First Amendment...had always meant that Congress was prohibited from establishing a national religious denomination — that Congress could not require all Americans become Catholics, Anglicans, or members of any other denomination. This understanding of "separation of church and state" was applied not only during the time of the Founders, but for 170 years afterwards.
>
> Then in 1962, the Supreme Court changed the definition of *church*. No longer would *church* mean a denomination; instead *church* now would mean a "religious activity." Therefore *separation of church and state* suddenly meant the complete separation of any religious activity from public affairs.[3]

God expects those who want His attention to pray. George Washington knew this and with his prayers brought miracles from the hand of God at Valley Forge and at many other times. The stained-glass window in the United States Congressional Chapel depicts our first president kneeling in prayer.

Yet the Bible and prayer are the most dangerous enemies in the world to dictators and other leaders who refuse to follow God. Corrupt government leaders know the only way the power of the Bible and prayer can be slowed down is to declare *both* illegal in their nations. Christians locked behind the Iron Curtain for seventy years discovered just how horrible such censorship really is.

Prayer is the strongest force against evil. But in 1962 the United States Supreme Court, which constantly declares itself the protector of free speech, impeded the free speech of every teacher and student by eradicating prayer from the classroom [*Engel v. Vitale*, 370 U.S. 421, 425 (1962)]. The prayer that was so horrible the courts said it must be stopped stated: "Almighty God, we acknowledge our dependence upon Thee, and we beg Thy blessings upon us, our parents, our teachers and our Country" [*Engel v. Vitale*, 370 U.S. 421, 422 (1962)]. The hypocrisy of this violation of free speech is obvious.

In 1963, the United States Supreme Court — which prides itself in opposing *all* censorship — agreed to censoring the Bible out of the hands of America's public schoolchildren. [*School Dist. of Abington Twp. v. Schempp*, 374 U.S. 203, 209 (1963)]. Our government claimed to be protecting the students by silencing God! In part, the ruling read: "If portions of the New Testament were read [to the students] they could be, and...had been, psychologically harmful to the child."[4]

The government removed no other book. Nor did they silence any other voice. Why were the Bible and prayer removed? Because the God who wrote the Bible — and listens to prayer — has declared Himself wiser than any human or source of intelligence on this planet. In fact, the God of the Bible has declared Himself the highest authority in the universe. And if there ever proves to be any other universe, He is God of that universe as well (John 1:3).

God, through His Word, claims higher authority than the president of the United States; higher authority than the United States Supreme Court; higher authority than the United Nations, NATO or any other human or man-made organization.

ABC television's "Nightline" host, Ted Koppel, was absolutely right when he said, "What Moses brought down from Mt. Sinai were not the Ten Suggestions. They are commandments."[5]

The Ten Commandments are the greatest law code ever written. Obeyed, they will keep people from immorality, stealing, committing murder, hating parents and so forth. But the courts in 1980 prohibited the Ten Commandments from being posted in any public school because if they "are to have any effect at all, it will be to induce the schoolchildren to read, meditate upon, perhaps to venerate and obey, the Commandments...[and] this...is not a permissible...objective."[6]

Yet the Bible declares that Jesus Christ is God. As one-third of the Godhead He came to earth in human form and died for every person who would declare Him Lord and follow His directions (Titus 2:13-14).

> Therefore also God highly exalted Him, and bestowed on Him the name which is above every name, that at the name of Jesus every knee shall bow...in heaven...on earth, and under the earth, and that every tongue shall confess that Jesus Christ is Lord, to the glory of God the Father (Phil. 2:9-11).

Again Christians had their free speech taken away in 1989 when the courts ruled that there could be no more prayer spoken prior to school athletic events so that no citizen would be offended by hearing the prayer.[7] Beer, however, can still be sold at any college or university football game no matter how many Christians are offended.

Censorship of the Bible was extended in 1989 in the declaration that a "school district acted properly in prohibiting a teacher from [silently] reading the Bible in...school classroom [during a silent reading period].[8]

The kids in America's public education system are bombarded daily by every evil that Satan can hurl their way. Yet parents, teachers and students are prohibited in the schools from sharing the answer that could liberate kids through a transformed life in Jesus Christ. Transformed kids are a plus!

Faith of Our Fathers

Our kids have the right to learn the rich heritage our founding fathers left for them regarding the necessity of prayer and the Bible. Imagine the impact the following quotes would have on today's world:

- George Washington: "It is impossible to govern the world without God."[9]

- John Quincy Adams: "So great is my veneration of the Bible that the earlier my children begin to read it, the more confident will be my hope that they will prove useful citizens to their country, and respectable members of society."[10]

- Patrick Henry: "There is a Book worth all other books which were ever printed."[11]

- Noah Webster: "The moral principles and precepts contained in the scriptures ought to form the basis of all our civil constitutions and laws...All the miseries and evils which men suffer from vice, crime, ambition, injustice, oppression, slavery, and war, proceed from their despising or neglecting the precepts contained in the Bible."[12]

- Thomas Jefferson: "I have always said, and I always say, that the studious perusal of the sacred volume [the Bible] will make better citizens, better fathers, and better husbands."[13]

- John Jay (first chief justice of the United States): "Providence has given to our people the choice of their rulers, and it is the duty as well as the privilege and interest of our Christian nation to select and prefer Christians for their rulers."[14]

- Abraham Lincoln: "This great Book [the Bible] is the best gift God has given to man.... But for it we could not know right from wrong."[15]

Does Prayer Change Things?

The youth of today would be inspired and should be motivated to model their lives and political actions set by our founding fathers in 1787. In *America: To Pray or Not to Pray* David Barton tells us:

> The early portion of the Constitutional Convention had been marred by dissension, hopeless deadlocks, and each state's unyielding adherence to its own selfish desires. The convention manifested all the markings of a complete failure...It was during this impasse that the nation's elder statesman and patriarch, Ben Franklin, rose to speak and quietly said:
>
> In the beginning of the contest with Britain, when we were sensible of danger, we had daily prayers in this room for Divine protection. Our prayers, Sir, were heard, and they were graciously answered. All of us who were engaged in the struggle must have observed frequent instances of a super-intending Providence in our favor...
>
> And have we now forgotten this powerful Friend? Or

79

do we imagine we no longer need His assistance? I have lived, Sir, a long time and the longer I live the more convincing proofs I see of this truth: "that God governs in the affairs of man." And if a sparrow cannot fall to the ground without His notice, is it probable that an empire can rise without His aid?

We have been assured, Sir, in the Sacred Writings that except the Lord build the house they labor in vain that build it. I firmly believe this. I also believe that without His concurring aid, we shall succeed in the political building no better than the builders of Babel; we shall be divided by our little, partial local interests; our projects will be confounded; and we ourselves shall become a reproach and a byword down to future ages. And what is worse, mankind may hereafter from this unfortunate instance, despair of establishing government by human wisdom and leave it to chance, war, or conquest.

I therefore beg leave to move that, henceforth, prayers imploring the assistance of Heaven and its blessing on our deliberation be held in this assembly every morning before we proceed to business.[16]

After this moving message, the entire Constitutional Convention did stop and pray. Barton writes,

Then they adjourned and for the next three days they prayed, attended church and listened to ministers challenge and inspire them...When they reassembled delegate Jonathan Dayton said: "Every unfriendly feeling had been expelled, and a spirit of reconciliation had been cultivated." The Constitution was written from that day.

President Harry S. Truman, thirty-third president of the United States, said:

The basis of the Bill of Rights comes from the teachings we get from Exodus and St. Matthew, from Isaiah and St. Paul. I don't think we can emphasize that enough these days. If we don't have a proper fundamental moral background, we end up with a...government which does not believe in rights for anybody except the State![17]

Christians need justice, not politics, at the Supreme Court today!

What Happens When You Close God Out?

Sophisticated America is so smart, so "beyond the need of God" that it has thrown the Bible out of its classrooms and evicted God from its life. Meanwhile, in many places churchgoers are like those described by Richard Halverson, former chaplain of the United States Senate, when he said, "At twelve o'clock each Sunday, the church yields up its dead!"

We live in a country where an estimated twelve million people acquire a venereal disease each year.[18] Where one in every eight women has been raped.[19] Where one in four citizens is a victim of crime each year.[20] By 1990 suicide ranked third in the causes of death for youth between the ages of fifteen and twenty-four.[21] And these are only tiny symptoms of our problems. Can we really believe we don't need God to change this?

Drop-outs

Nearly a million American high school students drop out of school every year. Maybe that drop-out rate is because kids are wising up. I asked one unsaved high school student why he dropped out of school, and he answered,

> "Because if, like my teachers tell me, there's no point in life — no exit except a lousy grave — why stay in school? I'll just live for now. I'll get everything I can while I'm still breathing."

Many Christians refer to their Bible as a compass. It points them constantly in the direction they should go. But when you're lost and there is no compass available, life becomes very confusing and frightening. Most students facing the twenty-first century are without "a compass."

The Good Old Days

How can we forget that America was made strong only because she recognized God as He blessed her? As a kid I remember singing "God Bless America" at every school assembly. Christmas carols proclaiming Jesus Christ were constant from the first grade on. Christmas vacation was Christmas vacation, not just "the holidays."

When I taught high school drama classes, I led my students in prayer before every play they performed. They were scared kids and realized they needed something beyond themselves just to get them on stage. Some of my students met Jesus Christ that way. Today millions of kids use drugs or alcohol in place of God to try to end their fears.

In the days I attended or taught school, the pledge of allegiance to the American flag started each day of school, and no one would have dreamed of leaving out those stirring words "one nation under God" (except the Jehovah's Witnesses, who were always excused from class until the pledge was over).

There was nothing strange about the Lord being part of our school life. America cut its teeth on the Bible. From our country's foundation and for more than the next hundred years, elementary schoolchildren learned to read by reading God's Word. The first colleges in our nation were Christian colleges. Prayer was constant. *McGuffey's Reader*, that included stories from the Bible, was the textbook for children in public grade schools. High school choirs sang glory to Jesus Christ without fear of being silenced by the ACLU or the Supreme Court.

Training Grounds

Christian parents want to know whether they can really trust the Bible always to give the right answers in life's choices for themselves and their kids. If the Bible isn't absolute, parents would be wrong to train their child by it.

If there is no right or wrong, then why point to the wrong "right"? If Christ isn't "*the* way, *the* truth and *the* life" (John 14:15), and there are other ways to get to God and heaven — or if there is no heaven — shouldn't all parents just let their kids do their own thing? Essential to deciding whether the Bible should be your guide in all of life's choices is the absolute certainty that the Bible is the truth, the whole truth and nothing but the truth.

Thomas Jefferson told us why the Bible is desperately needed in every segment of American society. He argued that mere law may or may not stop fleshly desires (immorality, stealing, murder and so on) and is not enough. Christ changes humans from the *inside.*

Jefferson said, "The precepts of philosophy, and of the [old legal] code, laid hold of actions only. [Jesus] pushed his scrutinies into the heart of man, erected his tribunal in the region of his thoughts."[22]

News Flash!

Ted Koppel, host of ABC's "Nightline," spoke to the 1987 graduating class of Duke University with these words:

> For moral absolutes, we have substituted moral ambiguity. We now communicate with everyone and say absolutely nothing. We have constructed the Tower of Babel, and it is a television antenna...We are beginning to make our mark on the American people. We have actually convinced ourselves that slogans will save us. Shoot up, if you must, but use a clean needle. Enjoy sex whenever and with whomever you wish, but wear a condom. "No." The answer is "no." Not because it isn't cool or smart or because you might end up in jail or dying in an AIDS ward, but "no" because it's wrong...I caution you, as one who performs daily on that flickering altar [of television] to set your sights beyond what you can see.[23]

If the Bible was just another book and God just one of many gods, I would have to advise all Christian parents to let their kids find their own way. But God isn't just another God on the block. He is King of kings and Lord of lords (Rev. 17:14). *All* kids have a deep need to know and be led by Him. So does every adult.

Throughout the rest of this book I will give parents careful and precise biblical directions for the training, disciplining and loving of their kids. But for the rest of this chapter I will outline why the Bible must be used above all other sources for the raising of their kids.

Does the Bible Offer Trustworthy Guidance?

Of all the proofs that the Bible is the inspired Word of God, none stands stronger than the fact that this book — completed two thousand years ago — *never* has to be corrected. Updating language usage sometimes makes translation a worthwhile endeavor. But the original texts remain original and forever true (2 Tim. 3:16-17).

Only those who would twist the Scriptures for their own purpose, or who really don't know what the Bible says in context, would dare to challenge God's Word. Any scholarly examination of the Bible (such as Bill Wilson's compilation of Josh McDowell's brilliant works, *A Ready Defense*) confirms that only the Holy Spirit could have given the Bible to mankind.

A Book or *the* Book?

> But know this first of all, that no prophecy of Scripture is a matter of one's own interpretation, for no prophecy was ever made by an act of human will, but men moved by the Holy Spirit spoke from God (2 Pet. 1:20-21).

Why were ten of the twelve men who followed Jesus Christ most closely willing to die hideous deaths of torture rather than denounce their Lord or His resurrection? The apostle John is generally believed to have died a natural death. But even Judas hung himself because he realized that Jesus was the Christ (Matt. 27:3-5).

Why in every century since the first has martyrdom been the way home for hundreds of thousands of Christians?

The apostle John stated:

> What was from the beginning, what we have heard, what we have seen with our own eyes, what we beheld and our hands handled, concerning the Word of Life — and the

84

life was manifested, and we have seen and bear witness and proclaim to you the eternal life, which was
with the Father and was manifested to us — what we have
seen and heard we proclaim to you also, that you also
may have fellowship with us; and indeed our fellowship
is with the Father, and with His Son Jesus Christ (1 John
1:1-3).

As we read these words today we tend to forget that they were
spoken and written during the first century. So many who read and
heard these words during the first century would have laughed the
apostles to scorn if they could have. Why didn't they do it? Because they, too, had seen Christ do what John and the others said
He did (Acts 26:26).

Archaeologists discover that ancient cities, peoples and artifacts
were located exactly where the Bible says they were. The Bible's
detail and accuracy are yet again confirmed when those who once
argued the nonexistence of these archaeological finds are proven
wrong.

Scientifically, the Bible makes total sense. A multitude of outstanding scientists are Christians and thoroughly believe all sixty-
six books of the Bible. They are amazed that any book finished
nearly two thousand years ago, written by people with dozens of
different occupations (from kings to fishermen), over a period of
several thousand years, cannot be scientifically scoffed at and
disproved today. Given our creator God, it is scientifically accurate
in every way. It was a research scientist from Stanford University
whom God used to lead me to Christ.

Prophetically, the Bible is totally accurate. The signs of the
times are everywhere (Matt. 24). "Impossible" predictions made
thousands of years ago are coming true today. Israel failed to exist as a
nation from 70 A.D. until 1947. In spite of the Jewish people being
scattered throughout all nations, God has preserved them and
brought them home (Jer. 23:8). Today every other country wants a
part of her. The final war in our world's history will soon be fought
in the valley of Armageddon (Rev. 16-19). Jesus Christ is coming
back soon.

Geographically, the Bible is totally accurate. Israel set her
boundaries by it.

Experientially, the Bible is totally accurate. If there is no Christ,

85

who is this living in my heart and in many millions of hearts the world over? How can we explain the miraculous transformation of millions of people who loved sinning and now feel deep sorrow any time they sin?

God answers prayer. Whenever our nation faces a crisis, even our president asks our nation to pray. By doing this he is recognizing who the greater authority really is. But if he didn't do this, he'd be a fool, because "the fool has said in his heart, 'There is no God' " (Ps. 53:1a).

Out on a Limb

The gigantic supernatural void left in the schoolroom by the removal of the Bible has been replaced with the other side of the supernatural. New Age thought, witchcraft and the occult are now being hyped as the "fun way" to know the future, amaze your friends, gather a crowd and make a fortune.

Your children are being introduced to crystals, astrology, astral-projection, Dungeons & Dragons, tarot cards and ouija boards in their schools. In an attempt to "motivate," "excite," "train" and "entertain," even major corporations are hiring occult teachers to train their troops in New Age practices.

> And when they say to you, "Consult the mediums and the wizards who whisper and mutter," should not a people consult their God? (Is. 8:19a).

Neither you nor your kids need crystals or gurus to predict your futures. God clearly promises to answer every question gladly (James 1:5-7). But remember that godly answers will *always* agree with biblical principles. God's spoken words will *never* disagree with His written Word (Josh. 1:8; John 15:7).

The final end for the followers of false religions or those who refuse to follow Christ will be the same:

> And the devil who deceived them was thrown into the lake of fire and brimstone, where the beast and the false prophet are also; and they will be tormented day and night forever and ever...This is the second death, the lake of fire. And if anyone's name was not found written in

the book of life, they were thrown into the lake of fire (Rev. 20:13,15).

Is it really difficult to determine whether telling the truth, living a guilt-free life and following the One who loves you most — or getting ripped off by the devil — is the better deal?

Brave New World?

So what has the government accomplished by kicking God out of our public schools? Drugs, alcoholism, suicide, gang violence, individual violence (including wife and husband beating), pornography, wife swapping, adultery, rape, incest, prostitution, bestiality, fornication, abortion, homosexuality, child abandonment, child abduction, child abuse, elder abuse and divorce have skyrocketed in America since 1962.

It is not the state that must be protected from the church but the church that must be protected from the state. The hideous tragedy of cult leaders such as Jim Jones, David Koresh and others, and the insane murder of their followers, will always be remembered by most Americans with great sorrow. But it is not these warped religious leaders who have done the most damage to the world. By far the most damage has been wrought by governmental leaders who have seized power, censored the living God and led with morally corrupt, mentally sick minds. These leaders become savage tyrants — from the Adolf Hitlers to the Joseph Stalins to the Idi Amins — murdering millions as they turn away from God.

Law and Justice for All

It is unconstitutional for a kindergarten class to recite: "God is great, God is good, let us thank Him for our food" (*Wallace v. Jaffree*, 1985).

In the Alaska public schools in 1987 students were told they could not use the word *Christmas* in school because it had the word *Christ* in it. They were told they could not have the word in their notebooks, exchange Christmas cards or presents, or display anything with the word *Christmas* on it. In Virginia a federal court has ruled that a homosexual newspaper may be distributed on a high school campus, but religious papers may not.[24]

In Omaha, Nebraska, ten-year-old James Gierke was prohibited from reading his Bible silently during free time...(or) to open his Bible at school and was told doing so was against the law.[25]

Teachers have to live in fear of being caught with a Bible in their possession. This isn't happening in Moscow. It is happening in the United States, which seems no longer to be "endowed by (its) Creator with certain inalienable rights," as the Declaration of Independence states.

Perhaps the finest Christian historian concerning all such matters today is David Barton. In his powerful book *The Myth of Separation*, Barton writes about the above kinds of incidents.

> Why were these activities never declared unconstitutional prior to 1947? The Constitution is still the same; yet, somehow, its meaning now appears to be different! This is because the 1947 *Everson v. Board of Education* (330 U.S. 1, 18) used an unprecedented legal manuever no previous court had ever dared to make. This (Supreme) Court took the Fourteenth Amendment as a tool to apply to the First Amendment *against* the states. Never before had the Fourteenth Amendment been used to forbid religious practices from the public affairs and public institutions of the individual states...The Fourteenth Amendment was ratified in 1868 to guarantee that recently emancipated slaves would have civil rights in all states. It is a strange interpretation that takes an Amendment providing citizenship to former slaves and uses it to prohibit religious activity in the schools or public affairs of any state....In *Walz v. Tax Commission*, 1970, the (Supreme) Court, in reviewing its use of the Fourteenth Amendment, admitted that by using the Amendment in such a manner, it had created an American revolution. The Court stated that this revolution "involved the imposition of new and far reaching constitutional restraints on the States. Nationalization of many civil liberties has been the consequence of the Fourteenth Amendment, reversing the historic position that the foundations of those liberties rested largely in state law."[25]

All who really care about these issues should carefully read David Barton's scholarly book, *The Myth of Separation*.

Yet God's voice is still being heard in the schools and courts — even the Supreme Court. Jay Sekulow, chief counsel of the American Center for Law and Justice (ACLJ), is leading some of the best Christian lawyers in America in arguing and winning case after case for Christians throughout this nation, even though the law is still very specific about prayer in public schools.

The ACLJ is a public-interest law firm and educational organization (located in the law and justice building at Regent University's law school in Virginia Beach, Virginia) focusing on pro-family, pro-life and pro-liberty issues. As I finish this book, they, like a SWAT team, are flying into cities and towns in all fifty states to stand up for Jesus Christ by *legally* defending the First Amendment free speech rights of kids. Multitudes of young people want to express their Christian beliefs through prayer at graduation ceremonies and other events or want to form and participate in non-curricular Bible clubs during off-hours at school. A nation that screams out constantly against censorship of any kind should certainly be screaming in favor of this.

What a contrast to the American Civil Liberties Union, which has declared that "student-initiated prayer is unconstitutional" and that school boards should reject organized efforts to include prayers in graduation ceremonies.[26]

If your children are harassed by teachers, principals or school boards, attacking them for praying, sharing their faith in Christ in a classroom or park, or for taking their Christian stand for God; or if you are threatened by an employer or employee because you do the same thing in your workplace, phone the center at 804-523-7570. They are spending their own money and the contributions of those who care to help people like you in these unbelievable situations.

Come Together, Christians!

Any government that can order the Bible out of schools or the workplace can order it out of the church.

In Russia and Germany, as in Rome, there came a day at different points in history when knocks came to the doors of people whom the government felt stood in the way of "progress." "Ethnic

89

cleansing" — happening even now in several places on our planet — began all at once and didn't stop until many millions had been tortured, murdered or placed in concentration camps because they dared to keep their faith or because they were born of the "wrong" race.

If the Christ-centered, Bible-believing pastors and people of America will repent, unite in prayer and purpose today to work together as one voice with letters and phone calls of encouragement and thanks to powerful people who stand for righteousness, and godly letters and phone calls of protest for those who don't, plus informed voting, we can stop abortion and stop losing all the religious privileges our forefathers fought so hard to give us. Christians have held these privileges dear since America was founded. We cannot lose them now if our kids are to follow Christ in a nation where their freedom will be honored.

Benjamin Franklin said, "If we do not hang together, we will all be hung separately!" There *is* still time to come together in Jesus' name. But there is not a lot of time. Lenin began with just seventeen turned-on communists. There are millions more Christians than that. The Bible declares, "Greater is He who is in you than he who is in the world" (1 John 4:4b). You and I can make the difference, especially as we raise godly children.

Written on a portion of the Berlin Wall inside East Germany was this statement:

"It is not to our shame this wall was built. It is to our shame we let this wall stand *after* it was built."

Dear Ray:

My whole family wants to ask you something — my wife, two sons, three daughters (and maybe the dog!). The kids range from three to midteen. We all want to "grow up in Christ" as you preached from Ephesians 4. Could you tell us how to grow up? Give us a list, Ray, of the things we could do individually and together that will help us become a mature family in Christ. Thanks.

A Whole Family Hungering and
Thirsting After Righteousness

Train up a child in the way
he should go, even when he is
old he will not depart from it.
Proverbs 22:6

FIVE

GOD WILL SPEAK TO YOUR KID IF YOU'LL LET HIM

*A thumbprint on the Bible
is more important than
a footprint on the moon.*

WHEN I WAS a teenager learning to drive, I would often sing the first stanza from my favorite song. It went:

This world is not my home; I'm just 'a passing through.
My treasures are laid up somewhere beyond the blue.
The angels beckon me from heaven's open door,
And I don't feel at home in this world anymore.

My dad would laughingly say, "Give me back the keys to my car or quit singing that song!"

But that song is still one of my favorites. Even if they never learn this song, your kids need to understand the heart of its message.

Every human has to choose one of two life views: one from the bottom, the other from the top. *Not* to choose is to choose anyway, because Jesus said, "He who is not with Me is against Me; and he who does not gather with Me, scatters" (Luke 11:23). Not to be a follower of Jesus Christ is to be going in the opposite direction.

First Things First

The Bible is not a difficult book to understand, nor is it too hard for a child to grasp. For more than the first hundred years of this nation, children basically learned to read by reading the Bible and stories from the Bible. That is a major reason why our nation held together even after 600,000 kids and men died during the Civil War.

"How can a young man keep his way pure? By keeping it according to Thy word" (Ps. 119:9).

Parents: Under Divine Appointment

God understands our kids far better than we do. He knows why He created them and how to bring them into the fullness of His plan for each of their lives. Yet in the same way that God the Father is the authority of God the Son (1 Cor. 11:3), you as a parent are the authority of your child or teenager (Eph. 6:1-4). God can choose to speak to your kid without your permission. But He deeply honors your divine appointment from Him as a parent and regards *you* as the most important person in your son or daughter's life as they grow up.

God will hold Dad most responsible for the training, discipline and love the child will need (Eph. 6:4). But it is the "parents" (Mom and Dad, not just Dad) whom the child is to "honor," which means to recognize as their first and foremost human authorities (Eph. 6:1).

The silly thing is that so many parents try to give their children training, love and discipline without using the Bible as their guidebook. So many Christians are righteously angry over the removal of the Bible from America's public schools, and yet they totally neglect it in their homes. Like the typical American, they're just "too busy."

Life on the Devil's Fast Track

Take a real look at family life on the fast track. Fathers are sacrificing time with their kids for business appointments. Over-tired mothers are coming home from outside employment with not enough money. Parents are so tired they ignore their kids or, even worse, abuse them mentally or physically.

Sex goes sour or dies between a husband and wife when she doesn't feel protected and cherished by him (Eph. 5:25) and he doesn't feel respected by her (Eph. 5:33).

Of course, it isn't only employed wives who are sometimes overtired. A day of worry can be more exhausting than a week of heavy work.

We live in a nation where one out of every two marriages ends in divorce. Two out of every five first marriages end in divorce. Sixty percent of second marriages end in divorce. Eighty percent of third marriages end in divorce. Ninety percent of fourth marriages end in divorce.

We can expect the above experiences from unchurched people. But one in three Protestant marriages and one in four Roman Catholic marriages are reportedly ending in divorce.

Kids on the Fast Track

Kids are watching the stability of their home life disintegrate before their eyes. Small wonder they end up looking for security and love in all the wrong places. One kid told me, "I think I'm more grown up than either of my parents." And when I met his parents, I didn't tell the kid, but I thought he was right!

The most important element in parenting is you, the parent or guardian of the kid. It is your Christian walk — your attitudes, habits, expressions, prayer life, love for God's Word and faith — that will have the most profound effect on your kids. These things will be picked up and mimicked by your children or teenagers.

Kids, especially teenagers, are extremely good at pinpointing hypocrisy in their parents. It's vital to maintain an honest walk with Christ if you want your kids to follow you to heaven.

My Box of Seeds

When I was twelve, Grandma Hicklin sent me a small box that I was to hang on my wall in my bedroom. In it was one page for each day of the year with the date, a Bible verse and a teaching that corresponded to the verse. Although I'd been to church a few times, I knew very little about the Lord. I certainly didn't know Him. But the pages in that little box somehow drew me to it nightly. Each page contained a Scripture passage for me to look up (kind of like a secret code and special message). At the bottom of the page was a reminder to pray for certain things, such as a country, my mother or dad, or my teacher.

That year was one of my best years as a kid. Mom said I was "tenderized" during that time. I was more loving and caring than I had been before. I prayed with a child's heart. But without deep roots the cares of this life blew me away for many years. I didn't know how much I needed Christ.

Grandma Hicklin never sent me another box like that, so when the year was over I quit praying nightly. But the respect for God's Word that I had gained never left me. In fact, I read the Bible through four times before I became a Christian at age thirty. To this day the Holy Spirit has been able to quicken Scripture passages to me that were planted during my lost years.

Jesus spoke of His Word as being "seeds" (Matt. 13:1-30). That's exactly what it is. Grandma Hicklin's box of "seeds" went down deep in me. Even if I had never been born again, I knew I could never get away from or deny the Bible. It is the book of books. It is awesome.

Family Devotions

It is rather easy to point children to Jesus Christ. Children are creatures of habit. When you form good habits in them very early, those habits are usually followed all the rest of their lives.

Train up a child in the way he should go, even when he is old he will not depart from it (Prov. 22:6).

Admittedly, teenagers who have grown like wild weeds in a home without Christ do present a bigger challenge when their parents are suddenly saved. A lot of what will happen at that point depends on the parental bond with those "weeds" up until that moment.

The parent who comes home from church and announces, "We

are now going to have three-hour family devotions every night!" will most likely be met with a Bronx cheer!

But even older teenagers in the home *can* and *do* come to Christ, often because they see Christ's love, joy, peace and discipline in the lives of parents who used to fall apart so often.

Let me suggest five powerful ways to interest your teenagers in Christ through videos:

1. Carman's *Time 2* videos, specifically geared to teach teens about God and the Bible. Adults will learn a great deal of answers for their teens' problems by watching these action-packed films too.

2. Carman's music videos. They are well done and "cool"!

3. Dennis Petersen's creation science videos, *Unlocking the Mysteries of Creation,* which will fascinate any teen or adult with science, archaeology, dinosaurs and an inspired creationist viewpoint. Dennis is the former curator of a museum and explodes scientific errors by bringing them into the light of the Bible.

4. My own Singles Plus seminar on video — ten and a half hours of teaching on dating, how to control the sex drive and the value of being single. The jokes alone will keep any teenager (or single person) laughing while they learn some of the most important truths in life. Married people laugh too!

5. James Dobson and Focus on the Family have wonderful resources: magazines, videos, audiotapes, even family devotion materials available to round out the Christian education of any age child or teenager. They have worked hard to keep everything Bible-based, Christ-centered and never boring.

God's Attitude Toward Family Devotions

God doesn't set up a biblical agenda for daily family devotions. It's different strokes for different folks.

Arlyne and I found what most people find today: Kids and parents are busy people with church, work, school, homework and individual pursuits. We began to understand God's plan in Deuteronomy 6:6-7:

> And these words which I'm commanding you today, shall be on your heart; and you shall teach them diligently to your sons and shall talk of them when you sit in your house and when you walk by the way and when you lie down and when you rise up.

God says it should be second nature for us to bring our best friend, Jesus Christ, into our conversations with our kids. Not in some forced way to impress them, or because it's the "religious" thing to do, but because kids of every age need to know God. They need to know His ways, not just His name. They need to understand how they personally fit into God's big picture. In short, they need to learn to follow Jesus. As a parent, you need to teach them the way.

A real Christian home is made up of people practicing the presence of Christ in their conversations and actions. It's where kids learn how natural and powerful prayer really is and where the family prays about everything that matters. It's where parents help their children to see how the Bible applies to daily situations and in crisis times as well.

Reading should be a regular part of home life. Arlyne nearly always reads children's devotional books and a Bible passage with our kids each morning before they went off to school. She often read from *The Living Bible* because it was easiest for them to understand when they were young. During their elementary years and into their teens, she read them wonderful Christian stories.

On our summer vacations in Oregon I read C. S. Lewis's *Chronicles of Narnia* to them. My kids loved it, especially since I did all the different voices of the various characters. Even in their teen years they wanted me to read that series aloud to them again.

Time spent driving somewhere was often used for reading too. Arlyne would drive, and I would read aloud stirring biographies and exciting stories of missionaries.

In 1977 my family and I spent a year ministering in New Zealand. While there I read aloud to them some great Christian books. With so little distraction from the boob tube (there were only two channels on television), they also began to read more books too.

After watching the news or a good program on television; while your kids are talking with you about a problem they are having; while looking at a tree with them; while building a bird house together — talk with them about the Lord and how the Bible relates to what you are seeing. Communicate in a natural, non-forced way.

Arlyne often taped Bible verses on the mirror in the kids' bathroom just to keep God's Word before their eyes. My kids, now adults, can still quote many of those verses today.

One tip: Be careful not to choose verses that will make them feel defensive, because they'll think you are preaching at them. Instead, you want them to love God and His Word.

King David explained why every kid needs to know the Bible intimately: "Thy Word have I hid in my heart, so that I might not sin against thee" (Ps. 119:11, KJV). Help your kids to "hide" God's Word in their hearts so they'll recognize right from wrong and choose to do things God's way.

Do Exactly What God Says to Do

The down payment of eternal life begins at salvation (John 10:10), and though the devil will try to steal it away, no Christian has to put up with him. As Christians we are directed to "Resist the devil and he will flee from you. Draw near to God and He will draw near to you" (James 4:7-8a).

Have you ever noticed that watching an exercise video does you no good unless you get busy and exercise? Promises like Isaiah 26:3 or James 4:7-8 are just words on a page until you "act upon them" (Matt. 7:2). That is, until you actually *do* what they say to do (James 1:22). When you teach your kids to *do* these things, and they do them, and you stay consistent with Christ in your own walk, your kids will most likely follow Christ enthusiastically the rest of their lives.

What God's Word *says* is validated by what God *does* when His directions are followed (John 7:16-17). That's why marriage always becomes fulfilling when the couple does what the Word says to do (Matt. 7:24-27). Kids find it fascinating to realize God's Word really works. The plan God has for them beats anything this world offers. The more they act on it, the more fulfilled they become.

Not Legalism or Sinless Perfection

Christianity is a lifestyle and a relationship, not a religion. "Religious" people think that doing or not doing certain things will determine whether or not they "earn" their wings for heaven. (I deeply enjoy watching the old Jimmy Stewart classic *It's a Wonderful Life,* but even angels don't get their wings for doing good deeds. Flight attendants do!)

It is essential that your kids learn right away the difference between grace and disgrace, legalism and illegalism. God doesn't want you or your children to become so heavenly minded you are no earthly good. Demanding perfection from your child will bring discouragement and will most likely cause him or her to rebel because of the frustration of not being able to live up to your demands.

A perfectionist is a person who takes great pains and gives them to others! The doctrine of "sinless perfection" — which says that once you know Christ you will be sinless or will learn to be sinless — is not only false but terribly destructive. The problem is that it can't be done.

Kids crash under the weight of legalism. And it has wiped out many otherwise godly men and women, too, who have never known the truth that would have set them free (John 8:31-32).

One of my best college friends is an avowed agnostic. Although the Lord gifted him with a great singing voice and acting talent, his legalistic parents believed performing on a high school stage was sinful, bringing attention to self rather than Christ. (Elvis Presley is said to have gone into the world to use his gifts because the people in his church attacked his talent the same way.) My friend had to "hide his talent under a bushel" until he finally rebelled and stopped going to church entirely. I see him once in a while, and we even talk about the Lord. But his parents' legalism on many matters turned him away from God a long time ago.

The Christian and Sin

The Bible never contradicts itself. Seeming contradictions evaporate by keeping Scripture passages in context. The apostle John had already confirmed the teaching of 1 John 3:6a in 1 John 2:1 and 4:

My little children, I am writing these things to you that you may not sin. But if anyone sins, we have an Advocate with the Father, Jesus Christ the righteous...The one who says, "I have come to know Him," and does not keep His commandments, is a liar, and the truth is not in him [or her].

Therefore:

1. If we really are born again we will make it a practice *not* to sin.

2. If we do stumble we can call on the Lord as we would call on a lawyer, and Christ will still rescue us out of sin.

3. We don't want to fall and will work diligently with Christ to keep His commandments.

4. If we say, after coming to Him, that it doesn't matter if we sin, we are a liar and not a Christian (1 John 1:6).

I have never forgotten the sad conversation I had aboard an airplane with a university sophomore. She had been "saved" at a church camp the summer before and told me she was going back to college "to sleep with several different guys." Then she said how glad she was that Jesus didn't care about it anymore and that now her conscience could "quit hurting."

When I showed her Scripture passages such as Romans 2:5-9; 1 Corinthians 6:9-11, 18-20; Ephesians 5:5-10; and Revelation 21:6-8, which implore the believer to turn away from sin, she said they told her at the camp that she was saved, and that was good enough for her. I weep at this kind of ignorance, but far more do I weep at the ignorance of those who misled her about salvation. They will have to answer to God for that false teaching (James 3:1).

Kids need to learn to have a repentant heart, get up, turn away from the sin, let the blood of Christ clean them up (1 John 1:5-9), work with God to avoid repeating the sin and keep on keeping on.

In spite of how tempting sin can be (Gal. 5:16), most kids would rather steal second base than steal a car. They love to be loved, admired and encouraged by a family that cares about them as a person. That's why Dad and Mom become so crucial in helping

101

them shape their own feelings about themselves. They know they will be a lot like you. So they want to know who you are, up close. Great parents have a strong tendency to produce great kids who turn into great adults.

Parents: You Are Not Alone

National studies show that the highest percent (some say as high as 85 percent) of people being born again are eighteen years old or younger. The mind-set and lifestyle of adults often make it far more difficult for them to open their hearts to Christ and follow Him, because receiving Christ does bring change. A kid is often far more ready to put Christ first than an adult is.

The most powerful place for Christlike transformation outside the home is the church and, specifically, the youth group at church. In great churches the senior pastor and youth leader have the same vision: to cause young people to become wise in the things of the Lord and to excite them with their potential in a world that needs Jesus Christ. In this way both the youth leader and pastor will "keep watch over your [kid's] soul" (Heb. 13:17a).

My oldest son, Tim, has a master's degree in youth ministry. He is currently youth pastor of the Foursquare Church in Pasadena, California. He is district youth representative for Southern California Foursquare churches. He also teaches courses on youth-related subjects at L.I.F.E. Bible College in Los Angeles. I asked Tim what a youth group should offer for maximum learning and growing in the Lord. Here is what he said:

> Have you ever stopped to ask yourself *that* question? If you have you're steps ahead of many parents who take for granted that "as long as my kids are in some kind of a church program, they're OK." While this would be an ideal, unfortunately, it is not always true. But the good news is that there are thousands of excellent youth ministries around the country. They don't all look the same, and they are not always found at the biggest churches in town. Let's take a look at what does set apart an excellent youth ministry from the others:
>
> 1. *It puts Jesus Christ first:* The number-one quality of

an excellent youth ministry is that it constantly brings students face-to-face with Jesus. The youth leaders take the spiritual lives of their students seriously, and they plan their ministry accordingly. This doesn't mean that a group won't be fun. (It should be!) But here are three questions that, when answered, will help you learn the priorities of a youth ministry: a) Is the group's teaching biblical, relevant and challenging? b) Does the group regularly engage its students in ministry to others? c) Do the students in this group *really* worship, or do they just have sing-alongs?

2. *It has strong leadership:* Churches that are desperate to find "anyone willing to work with our youth" will rarely have excellent youth ministries. Often these churches settle for whomever they can "get" rather than praying, searching and waiting for excellent leaders. Over and over in the New Testament Paul exhorted the believers to "imitate me" and "follow my example." Your young people *will* become like those who lead them. Ask yourself this important question: Would it be OK for my kids to turn out like these youth leaders?

3. *It is filled with Christ's love:* Another quality that is shared by excellent youth ministries is that they are places where young people know they are loved. Kids are not easily fooled by phonies — they *know* when love is real! They will feel loved when they are unconditionally accepted by leaders and peers, when they are listened to and when they aren't allowed to do "just as they please" but rather are lovingly challenged to do what is right.

This isn't to say that your kids will feel loved and accepted from the instant they walk in the door. Often students have their defenses up because of their own insecurities. They need to be encouraged to stick it out for a month or so, to give the group a fair chance. This also isn't to say there will never be relational difficulties and misunderstandings. Adolescents are learning how to survive socially as adults. But their inexperience can lead them to make frequent, often painful, blunders! Encourage students not to give up easily on the healthy relationships they have built.

The kid who misses out on being part of a youth group like the one Tim just described is a kid who will have a deep void in his or her growing up years, in spite of having great parents.

A church should offer young children more than a place to play. There are some dynamic church programs throughout our country that are powerfully ministering to young children from the time they can crawl until they enter the junior high group. These children's Sunday school classes and programs offer a wide variety of teaching and activities that can help you train up your children in the way they should go. They contain the central elements Tim listed for junior high and high school youth, geared to a child's level. No child is "too young" to become part of a Christ-centered, Bible-directed church and children's program.

Christian Bookstores

A tract next to your teenager's lasagna, if he or she doesn't know the Lord, will probably go unread. But good Christian music, excellent Christian magazines, great Christian cassettes, CDs and videos can be powerful forces against hell in your house. Many a teenager has met Christ because a song or story tenderized his heart.

Not all books in Christian bookstores are necessarily Christian or worth reading. Store owners can only make available what they hope and pray will be the best books for you and your kids. That's why *you* as the parent need to plan a day about every three months to spend some quality time at a Christian bookstore. Browse. Take real time. When they are old enough to handle books well, teach your children to do the same.

Ask yourself these questions in choosing a Christian book:

1. Is it biblical? As I skim through the pages of this book, am I seeing teaching that I know to be true? If

it contains things I am just learning, how much Scripture is in the book that I can check with my own Bible? (Acts 17:11).

2. Is it interesting to me? As you skim through the pages of a book, ask yourself: Will I read this book once I get it home? Book publishing companies are well aware that certain book covers attract buyers. But don't buy a book for its cover; buy it for its *content.*

Learn the names of authors who do a great job with every book they write. James Dobson, Josh McDowell, Jack Hayford, Patrick Morley, Chuck Swindoll, Gary Smalley and C. S. Lewis are among my favorite authors for adults. What you learn from them will help your child because it will help *you* grow in Christ.

If you want to know how America is doing, read Pat Roberton's latest. He is undoubtedly the foremost Christian news analyzer alive today. (Try not to miss "The 700 Club" on TV every weekday or weeknight. It will do your whole family good.)

If you want to get your finances in order, teach your kids how to handle money or learn still more about the state of our union, read books by Larry Burkett.

Teen-Geared Books and Books for Children

There are lots of excellent books written for teenagers these days. Among the best authors for teens are Ken Davis, Winkey Pratney, Dawson McAllister, Lorraine Peterson and the amazing Josh McDowell. Some of the best series of novels are by authors Frank Peretti and Judy Baer, and one by several different authors, the Christy Miller Series.

Kids ages eight to twelve will want books by these authors: Lois Gladys Leppard, Frank Peretti, Lee Roddy and Hilda Stahl. And check out the brilliantly written Choice Adventures Series.

Children under eight will thrill to *Little Visits With God* and *More Little Visits With God* by Allan Hart Jahsmann and Martin Simon; *The Beginner's Devotional* by Stephen T. Barclift; and *Every Day With God: A Child's Daily Bible* by Word. Christian bookstores offer many wonderfully illustrated books that will fascinate young minds.

Focus on Your Family

A section on the best of Christian resources could never be complete without again mentioning James Dobson and Focus on the Family. His office will keep you *in focus* on the current best in every category. The "Adventures in Odyssey" series on videos, cassettes and CDs is enough to make Hollywood drool! Dobson claims these stories are for kids, but Arlyne and I don't want to leave the car when "Adventures in Odyssey" is on the air. And that's one more tip: When you're traveling in the car with your kids (including teenagers), have Christian cassettes or CDs available. Whenever Christian radio doesn't please the whole family, pop in a Christian tape that will.

Remember that no book by any author is meant to replace daily Bible study. The only way to keep your family free of deception, and yourself free of error, is to "study to show yourself approved by God" (2 Tim. 2:15).

Neighborhood Bible Clubs and Teen Missions

If you'd like to see the kids on your block meet Jesus and have their lives transformed, why not look into the possibility of holding a Christian club for children in your neighborhood? Talk that over with your pastor.

Meanwhile, what teenager doesn't dream of getting away to far-off places for a whole summer? It can be done. Arlyne and I believe this is one of the best weaning experiences available to families. Teen Missions will train and send your teenager, along with other Christian teens from all over America, overseas for a full summer of Christian service. Teenagers from their thirteenth year on can go. (A month-long program in the United States is available for kids ten years old and over.)

Teen Missions instructs and assists kids in raising their own missionary support so that it doesn't break you financially to send them. The hard missionary work the teenagers do in Jesus' name will be worth all the contributions from you, your friends and your church. The teenagers dig ditches, mix mortar, lay bricks, build orphanages, churches and youth camps, sing in churches and evangelize in the countries to which they are sent. They are trained in how to do all these things during an intensive two weeks of early summer training in Merritt Island, Florida. They also run a daily obstacle course with their team which includes climbing a twelve-foot wall and using a rope-swing across a swamp. They have marvelous Bible studies and grow as Christians.

Our kids were all part of Teen Missions in their teen years. When Elizabeth was fifteen, she spent a full summer with them in Germany. David started at fourteen by going to France. The next summer he was in communist Poland *before* the Iron Curtain was torn down. At fifteen, Tim was startled when he got his first assignment — to the Amazon jungle of Brazil! He loved every minute of that summer. During his second summer he went to Germany.

It's always best to check with your own pastor and youth leader to discover opportunities not mentioned here. There are many. No young person need spend a wasted summer when he or she can serve the Lord.

If you want some of the best biblical training in the shortest time attend a Youth With a Mission Discipleship Training School. Your whole family can attend a Youth With a Mission Discipleship Training School. Discipleship Training Centers are located in more than a hundred cities and towns throughout America and the world. There are three-month schools, followed by two months of field instruction and training, teaching everyone from tot to ninety how to share their faith in Christ easily with everyone. Attending a mini-discipleship training course gave me one of the best jump-starts in ministry a Christian could receive. Phone YWAM at 1-800-922-2143, and have them send you a *Go Manual*. Then take your family and *go!* Your whole family will be glad you did.

Getting the Right Start

Kids need elementary school before they are sent to high school or college. Servicemen are sent to boot camp before they are sent to war. Before we can be licensed to drive, we are required to take both a written and a physical driving exam. In just such a way, the child or new believer should be taught Christian basics. A proper foundation of biblical knowledge will make them much stronger in their walk with Christ. Without having these truths imbedded in their spirits, it is easy for them to be seduced by "every wind of doctrine" (Eph. 4:14).

Here are five basics for every Christian home:

1.   Teach your family to believe the Bible (John 8:31-32):

And without faith it is impossible to please Him, for he who comes to God must believe that He is, and that He is a rewarder of those who seek Him (Heb. 11:6).

God cannot lie (Titus 1:2). Lies come only from the devil (John 8:44) and from those following or being used by him (Rom. 1:25). Therefore, "Forever, O Lord, Thy Word is settled in heaven" (Ps. 119:89). You and your kids can totally trust the Word of God because *it will never change.* In a fast-changing world, you have Someone you can totally rely on who will never let you or your kids down as you trust in Him.

Your kids need to learn to walk with Christ in real faith. But remember that "without faith it is impossible to please God" (Heb. 11:6a). God loves them (and you) and cannot bless each member of your family unless you each follow Him individually.

True, you won't always understand His ways. (I've had several arguments with God and have lost every one!) I don't know why He doesn't make the stoplights of life change faster or why life is terribly unfair at times. We see things only with *our* eyes. God sees the big picture. We're in sales; He's in management!

Isaiah says that God's thoughts are not our thoughts, neither are His ways our ways (Is. 55:8). Any sincere study of the Bible will produce real answers to many of life's biggest mysteries.

The true, rich blessings of God flow through those who believe Him (Heb. 11:6b). Believing God means recognizing His sovereign lordship. "Faith is the assurance of things hoped for, the evidence of things not seen" (Heb. 11:1). If you can see the result right now, it requires no faith. I'm *not* referring here to positive thinking. Positive thinking isn't what rescued Daniel from the lions (Dan. 6). Daniel had faith that God would think positively for the lions!

Faith says, "God told me to do something. Fast and pray for me. If I perish, I perish" (see Esth. 4:16b).

Faith says, "If you can't stand the heat, don't go into the kitchen. But I know what God told me to do, and I'm going in!" (see Dan. 3:16-30).

Faith rejoices and sings praises to God in the midst of trials —

even unfair trials (Acts 16:22-25; Phil. 4:4; James 1:2-4).

In great faith:

> Women received back their dead by resurrection; and others were tortured, not accepting their release, in order that they might obtain a better resurrection; and others experienced mockings and scourgings, yes, also chains and imprisonment. They were stoned, they were sawn in two, they were tempted, they were put to death with the sword; they went about in sheepskins, in goatskins, being destitute, afflicted, ill-treated (men of whom the world was not worthy), wandering in deserts and mountains and caves and holes in the ground. And all these, having gained approval through their faith (Heb. 11:35-39b).

Faith believes the Bible no matter what happens (Rom. 10:17). Faith knows this world is not our home; we're just passing through (Phil. 3:20). Faith is content every day because it is following the Lord wherever He leads (Phil. 4:11). Faith knows there is a purpose in *all things*, no matter how they look at the moment, and that purpose ultimately is going to work "good" for the one who has faith (Rom. 8:28). Faith expects a miracle, and it brings great rewards from God (Heb. 11:6b). Your kids need to learn faith like this from you.

2. Teach your family about water baptism (Rom. 6:4-6, 10).

God's first requirement for a new Christian is to be water baptized (Mark 16:15; Acts 2:38). Water baptism is far more than a symbolic act. It is an act of obedience and identification with Christ as His follower. Water baptism breaks the power of sin as the Christian rises out of the water with new ability to follow Him. It offers a profound spiritual moment of deliverance.

In the words of Paul:

> For if we have become united with Him in the likeness of His death, certainly we shall be also in the likeness of His resurrection...Even so consider yourselves to be dead to sin, but alive to God in Jesus Christ (Rom. 6:5, 11).

When is a child old enough to be water baptized? As soon as he or she receives Christ, understands water baptism and then really wants to be baptized — not just when he or she is "talked into it." Wait until your child really wants to identify with Jesus Christ this way.

Just before my family left for our year of ministry in New Zealand, all of my children were water baptized at the Church on the Way. It was a magnificent experience for each of them and for Arlyne and me. The power of their identification with Christ was vital, and it remains so to this day.

Each of our children had received Christ when they were very young. Our delay in allowing Tim to be water baptized was not at all because of his lack of desire toward it. We had simply been fearful that Tim might not appreciate it as much as he would if he were "old enough." He was profoundly affected by the experience at age twelve. But so was Elizabeth at age eight, and David at age six.

3.   Teach your family to serve the Lord (Eph. 2:8-10).

My dad had just one definition for love, and he repeated it over and over again. Dad said, "Love is service." In all the years I've taught on love I have never found a better definition (Heb. 6:10; Eph. 2:8-10; John 14:15).

When you serve God fully with joy in your heart, nothing is more thrilling than to see your kids excited about what Jesus Christ is doing in their lives. When your kids *want* to serve Him, your joy knows no bounds.

I have seen some kids get excited about Jesus only to have their parents squelch their joy. What started out as release from drugs, immorality or even boredom for one bright, flickering moment gave real hope to the kids. Life took on meaning. But then their parents (even some Christian parents) insisted they stay home from church to do anything from chores to homework. Or they punished their kids by grounding them from youth group. The parents told them, "Don't get carried away with all this Christian stuff. This is a *real* world we live in, and you're going to have to get top grades to go to college."

Both chores and homework are important (Luke 10:38-42). But these parents either don't know or have forgotten what Jesus said:

So don't worry at all about having enough food and

clothing. Why be like the heathen? For they take pride in all these things and are deeply concerned about them. But your heavenly Father already knows perfectly well that you need them, and He will give them to you if you give Him first place in your life and live as He wants you to (Matt. 6:31-33, TLB).

Giving Christ first place means serving Christ. But *service* needs to be redefined. Too many think of "full-time Christian service" as pastoring or doing missionary work. Not so. Although full-time Christian service includes both these things, many a mechanic, secretary, doctor, garbage collector or pilot is in "full-time Christian service" too. In fact, for a Christian, all work is a calling, because "the steps of a good man [or woman] are ordered by the Lord" (Ps. 37:23). The "church service" should begin when people go out the door of a church.

Kids serve Christ by doing their work "heartily, as for the Lord rather than for men" (Col. 3:23b). That's true whether they're doing work around the house or yard, working in a store or gas station or doing research for a term paper. Honesty, energy, enthusiasm and hard work without complaint are contagious. Those who lack these characteristics often ask the ones who have them *how* they got them. Explaining how is the very best form of witnessing (Acts 1:8).

To know Christ is to love Him. We *serve* Him because we *love* Him. Love is service.

4. Teach your family about the power of prayer and the laying on of hands (Mark 16:17-18).

Prayer and the laying on of hands were not new ideas Christ taught. Many incidents of laying on hands for God's purposes are found throughout the Old Testament (Gen. 48:14; Ex. 29:10,15,19; Lev. 4:15; Deut. 34:9). But what was new with the coming of Christ was the power (the Greek word *dunamis*) that came from His hands.

A passage in Habakkuk described the awesome power of God's ministry through Christ's hand. It is somewhat obscured in the King James Version because the Hebrew word for "horn" and "hand" is the same. Thus, the King James Version talks of the power coming from His "horn." More modern translations have corrected this interpretation. Here it is in the New American Standard Bible:

God comes from Teman, and the Holy One from Mount Paran. His splendor covers the heavens, and the earth is full of His praise. His radiance is like the sunlight; He has rays flashing from His hand, and there is the hiding of His power (Hab. 3:3-4).

Christ fulfilled this prophecy. "His radiance is like the sunlight" — God kept Peter and John from being blinded during the transfiguration of Christ (Matt. 17:2; Mark 9:2-3). "He has rays flashing from His hand, and there is the hiding of His power" — Jesus Christ continually healed those with sicknesses and deformities, cast out demons, raised the dead and "cleansed" the lepers to wholeness through the laying on of His hands (Matt. 8:3; 9:29; 20:34; Mark 6:2,5; 8:23; Luke 4:40; 7:14; 13:13).

But our Lord did not keep this power of healing to Himself (Matt. 9:36; 10:1). Nor did He limit His healing power to the twelve (Luke 10:1,9).

Jesus Christ is the same yesterday, today, yes and forever (Heb. 13:8).

This is not a book about healing. Every denomination or independent church has its own teaching regarding this subject. But does it make sense to think that our compassionate Lord would only care to heal the sick during the three and a half years of His earthly ministry?

A dramatic example of healing is given in Acts 3:1-18. Peter was on his way to a prayer meeting when he touched a lame man and healed him. The crowd was ecstatic, and Peter seized the moment to preach salvation through Jesus Christ. But the Sanhedrin, the highest human religious power of its day, was furious. They arrested Peter and John (Acts 4:1-7).

Undeterred, Peter preached Christ at his trial (Acts 4:8-12). Unable to deny the fact of the miracle because the healed man stood before them, the Sanhedrin tried to silence Peter and John with a warning never to speak the name of Jesus again (Acts 4:13-18). Peter and John said they could not help but speak about Him (Acts 4:19-20). It is the stirring prayer of Peter and John that should speak to you and your family today:

"And now, Lord, take note of their threats, and grant that Thy bond-servants may speak Thy word with all confidence, *while Thou dost extend Thy hand to heal, and signs and wonders take place* through the name of Thy holy servant Jesus." And when they had prayed, the place where they had gathered together was shaken, and they were all filled with the Holy Spirit and began to speak the word of God with boldness (Acts 4:29-31, italics added).

In 1970 I was healed of cancer because a friend of mine laid hands on me and asked Jesus Christ to heal me. He prayed a very simple prayer. The next morning I went to the hospital for surgery and was sent home. The cancer was gone. It has never returned.

In 1980 I developed a very painful right wrist. Though I prayed about it, the pain remained. Finally my doctor told me I had carpal tunnel syndrome, a nerve disorder in my wrist that would get much worse. He said, "When it gets so bad you can't tolerate the pain even with aspirin, come back for surgery. I'll have to scrape the nerves."

I went home in pain. When our sixteen-year-old Tim heard what was wrong, he said, "Dad, I don't believe Jesus Christ wants you to have that pain. Let me pray for you." He laid his hand on my wrist and prayed. Instantly the pain was gone. It has never returned.

Expect miracles from Jesus Christ in your own home through prayer and the laying on of hands. We don't need New Age — we need the Rock of Ages. God is not anti-doctor. Luke the physician wrote two great books of the Bible. And there is nothing wrong with an aspirin if you need it. "A merry heart doeth good like a medicine" (Prov. 17:22, KJV). But it is Jesus Christ, not some aspirin brand, who has "the name above every name" (Phil. 2:9). Reach for Him before you reach for anything else (2 Chron. 16:12-13).

I urge every Christian family to expect the Holy Spirit to be far more present in their day-to-day lives. God is the God of miracles (Heb. 13:8).

5.   Enlarge your family's heavenly view (2 Pet. 3:9-12).

Set your mind on things above, not on the things that are on earth (Col. 3:2).

This life of ours is but a drop in the ocean of eternity. Its disappointments will evaporate in the glory of the future when we fix our eyes upon Christ (Is. 26:3.)

> And do not fear those who kill the body, but are unable
> to kill the soul; but rather fear Him who is able to destroy
> both soul and body in hell (Matt. 10:28).

Understanding the reality of heaven and hell will help your kids want to stay away from sin (James 4:7-8). Earth is the land of the dying. Heaven is the land of the living. Your kids need to realize this as soon as possible.

Is heaven a real place? Yes. Otherwise Jesus Christ is a liar or a lunatic. He certainly has been the reason why millions died in martyrdom. And thus, unless He's the living Lord, He is the mass murderer of more lives than any other person in history — and never should be worshipped.

Some people are locked up for saying they are God. But that's exactly who Jesus said He was (John 14:1-3, 6-7). And the things He said and did proved He was and is God (Phil. 2:5-11).

Even death holds no victory over the Christian because "death is swallowed up in victory" (1 Cor. 15:54b). The grieving family and friends at a funeral may not think that way as they look into a coffin at someone they love. Of course they grieve, but the grieving is for themselves, they who have been temporarily left behind. If the person who used to live in that body is a Christian, he or she has just embarked on the greatest adventure of their lives, and it will continue forever! That person will be with Jesus Christ and loving every second forever! "And this is the promise which He Himself made to us, the eternal life" (1 John 2:25).

Heaven

There *is* a city with no smog — in fact, no bad weather at all. It is totally free of sickness and crime and totally moral, and it offers nothing but mansions to its residents, free of charge forever. It has the greatest leader in government who will reign there eternally. You and your kids will love it. And you can live there forever, tax-free!

114

And I saw the holy city, new Jerusalem, coming down out of heaven from God, made ready as a bride adorned for her husband. And I heard a loud voice from the throne, saying, "Behold, the tabernacle of God is among men, and He shall dwell among them, and they shall be His peoples, and God Himself shall be among them, and He shall wipe away every tear from their eyes; and there shall no longer be any death; there shall no longer be any mourning, or crying, or pain; the first things have passed away." And He who sits on the throne said, "Behold, I am making all things new." And He said, "Write, for these words are faithful and true." And He said to me, "It is done. I am the Alpha and Omega, the beginning and the end. I will give to the one who thirsts from the springs of the water of life without cost. He who overcomes shall inherit these things, and I will be his God and he will be My son [or daughter]" (Rev. 21:2-7).

Is Hell a Real Place?

Once again, Jesus Christ would be a monstrous liar or a lunatic if there is no eternal hell. He convinced multitudes of people who have lived under torture or died for Him that they are to fear hell enough to keep on living for Him (Matt. 10:28). Like many others, Arlyne came to Christ when she was a young girl because of this fear.

Christians know where they will spend eternity. And no matter what it costs in this life, it will be well worth the sacrifice for what we will both gain and miss. We will gain heaven, but we will miss a hell of "unquenchable fire...where their worm does not die, and the fire is not quenched" (Mark 9:43b, 48).

God created hell for Lucifer, who pridefully attempted to wrest control of heaven and take the highest throne and be as God (Is. 14:12-17; Rev. 12:7-9). All who follow him instead of Christ will be cast into hell with him (Rev. 20:10-15).

Jesus Christ warned mankind more about hell than He told them about heaven.

For God so loved the world that He gave His only begotten Son, that whosoever believes in Him should not perish, but have eternal life (John 3:16).

Even a small kid can comprehend that if there really were no hell, then Adolf Hitler, Joseph Stalin, Idi Amin and all other butchering dictators would have gotten off scot-free. If Hitler, after gassing millions of Jews, simply put a gun to his head one day, pulled the trigger and went to sleep forever with no consequence for his heinous crimes, *that* would be hell for the rest of us! But the God who wrote the Bible and *never lies* (Titus 1:3) tells us there is a hell. Any man or woman who sins with their words, thoughts or actions will die, now or later. Christ is their only way out (John 14:6). The worms remain hungry. And there is a coming day of judgment (Rev. 20:12-15).

A mother recently asked if we should perhaps avoid speaking about hell to our children because the idea is too frightening. But if your child had a cancerous tumor and a doctor knew that removal of the tumor would save your child's life, would the doctor be "frightening" your child to offer surgery? Of course not. Hell is a real place. God loves you and your kids enough to have sent Christ to die for each of you so that, by receiving His only Son, you would never have to go there (John 3:16).

> The Lord is...not wishing for any to perish but for all to come to repentance (2 Pet. 3:9).

> For the Lord searches all hearts, and understands every intent of the thoughts. If you seek Him, He will let you find Him; but if you forsake Him, He will reject you forever (1 Chron. 28:9).

Once Christians know Jesus Christ *is* God, they live to follow Jesus Christ *as* God. If all it takes to be a Christian is to know Christ, every demon in hell is saved, because "the demons also believe, and shudder" (James 2:19). They shudder because they know they're going to spend eternity in hell (Rev. 20:10, 14-15). The tragedy is that many humans who don't follow Christ aren't even smart enough to shudder!

Christians never meet
for the last time.

Dear Ray:

My ten-year-old son, Nick, just called me a liar! I spanked him and sent him to his room. Now I've sat down at the dining room table to ask you some questions.

First, is my son right? I told him last week I'd take him to a Cowboys game tomorrow night. But today a friend asked my wife and me to dinner tomorrow night, and I accepted. My son was really upset when he found out. My wife got mad at me too!

Second, I have taken our other two kids to the Cowboys games, but not Nick. Nick is handicapped, and I'm a bit concerned about his having to climb the stadium steps. What do you think?

Hung by My Tongue

And my God shall supply
all your needs according to
His riches in glory
in Christ Jesus.
Philippians 4:19

SIX

What Does Your Kid Really Need?

"My name is Jimmy.
I want all you'll gimmee."

AUNT CLARISSA HAD brought two identical candy bars to Hetzebel and her little brother Throckmorton. She held both out to Hetzebel and asked, "Which one do you want?" Without hesitation Hetzebel said, "I want *his!*"

In a land of Nintendo, ballet lessons, Tae Kwon Do and Little League, it is hard for kids to decide exactly what they want to do. Piano lessons can be expensive, yet kids often make it a practice *not* to practice. Still, if a friend is taking lessons or if Throckmorton watches Dino Kartsonakis on TBN one day, he may easily think, I want to play like that too! If Dad or Mom is an easy touch, he may be starting lessons within the week — and quitting after three months of tug-of-wars trying to get Throckmorton to the piano bench!

An "easy touch" for the kids — that's the problem. But if Dad and Mom were an "easy touch" for the Holy Spirit, praying and seeking God for answers about raising their kids, they wouldn't make decisions simply to satisfy childish whims. Instead God could direct the family. So much time, money and tears would be spared for things that really mattered. And God's will would be done.

Many parents believe it is their duty to wean their children from dependence on them to complete dependence on themselves, making their kids completely independent. But independence should never be the goal.

Instead, children need to grow from complete dependence on the parent to complete interdependence (we all need one another) and ultimate dependence on Christ. Thus the maturing child will learn to follow the same leadership as his or her parent follows. Both the child and the parent will learn to get their orders from God.

Needs Versus Wants

In Philippians we read the promise:

> My God shall supply all your needs according to His riches in glory in Christ Jesus (4:19, italics added).

That promise was given to the Philippian Christians, the largest contributors to the apostle Paul's ministry (see Phil. 4:15-18). Yet the book of Philippians isn't just a donor letter — it is Scripture. The Philippians weren't being given a simple promise of having only their needs met. They had entered into a special giving of themselves through their money, which they continued to give Paul to help advance Christ's kingdom (Phil. 4:16,18). Therefore, Paul guaranteed they would receive supplies for all their needs according to Christ's heavenly riches.

This is no get-rich-quick scheme. But because the Philippian Christians gave gladly, they would be blessed mightily by the Lord with His riches. The biblical word *riches* must never be reduced to simply meaning "money." It does include money, but God's riches are blessings however needed — love, joy, peace, wholeness and the blessings that richly fulfill a Christian in every area.

Treat your children and teenagers as God treats you, His child. As they grow you will work to meet their *needs* — food, shelter and clothing. They can expect that because they are your kids.

Then as they become contributors to the family through loving cooperation and obedience, you will go much further. As your children relate to you with respect and love and seek to satisfy your unselfish requests (emptying the garbage, mowing the lawn, dusting, taking care of pets, washing dishes), you will do much more than meet their needs.

You will even seek, whenever it wouldn't harm them spiritually, to fulfill their wishes with your riches. This is bonding at its best. It is essential for every happy home. It is also a picture of God's loving relationship with us, His children.

You will also discipline them when they rebel. "For those whom the Lord loves He disciplines" (Heb. 12:6a). You will discipline them *because you love them.*

The needs of your kids can best be met by you — their parent or guardian. Meeting these needs causes a powerful bonding btween you. Once that bonding includes Jesus Christ in the center of it, almost nothing can remove it. The purpose of the next three chapters will be to list ten of the very biggest needs your child or teenager has. If you fail to meet these ten needs, your child (often as a teenager) will most likely rebel from you. He or she may even try to break your heart.

1. Needed for bonding: parents who make love, not war.

> Wives, be subject to your husbands, as is fitting in the Lord. Husbands, love your wives, and do not be embittered against them (Col. 3:18-19).

The deep belief that his or her parents are in control is essential to wholeness in any child. Thus they'll find security and joy — and little fear — in their formative years (Rom. 14:17).

The greatest peace and joy arrives when a child comes under the lordship of Jesus Christ, the One in control of his or her parents. As the child learns to follow Him, he will have God's powerful protections and blessings throughout his childhood, no matter what temporary blips come across his happiness screen (Gal. 5:22-23).

But when parents constantly scream at each other or the child or are violent, they prove they are out of control. When both parents are often out of control, the child finds the world a very insecure place in which to live.

I Haven't Always Known This

If you have read my book *Marriage Plus* or attended one of my seminars, you know I wanted a divorce for the first twelve years of my marriage. Arlyne and I had "irreconcilable differences," and I didn't believe anything could ever be done to fix them. Divorce seemed the logical way out. Thank God I didn't take it. What a waste of our lives, and our kids' lives, that would have been.

I was born again during the eighth year of our marriage. But that alone was not enough to release us from our pain. I almost left my wife for someone else during the tenth year. Again Christ pulled me out of the pit and would not let me go. But not until a dozen years of an earthly hell went by did Arlyne and I discover God really is the God of the impossible (Luke 1:37).

It was the Bible that set us free (John 8:31-32). This began during a two-month time of plunging into the Word and studying everything I could find regarding the husband's role, the wife's role, finances, sex, communication and rearing kids. I discovered over a thousand verses giving full directions on these subjects. I was set free and able to help set Arlyne free. Suddenly our kids were set free too.

Scared Kids

Whether Big Brother is watching you or not, your Hetzebel and Throckmorton are!

Our own son, Tim, was developing an ulcer at the age of four because of the way Arlyne and I were verbally tearing each other apart. When Tim was six years old, I asked him, "What was it like for you when your Mommy and I used to fight?"

Tim answered, "Well, you'd start yelling at Mommy, and she'd start yelling at you. You'd get louder and louder. I'd be lying on my bed and start shaking 'cause I was scared. I wondered who was going to leave me. Was my mommy going to leave me? Or was my daddy going to leave me? And I didn't want *either* of you to leave me. Finally I'd be shaking so hard I'd pull the covers over my head, and I'd shake underneath them!"

My actions caused that response in my four-year-old son. There's no excuse for it. But I'm so glad the Lord heals and cleanses (1 John 1:9).

Shortly after the day Tim shared this with me, I took him on my lap and asked him to do something for me.

He said, "Sure, Dad, what?"

"Would you forgive me, son?" I asked him.

I had written down ten episodes where Tim had been involved either directly or indirectly. I knew he'd been emotionally wounded each time. I briefly described each incident to him. It was no surprise to me that he remembered every one of them. After each description I'd ask, "Would you forgive me for that?

Each time he replied, "Sure, Dad. I forgive you."

My son got off my lap a brand-new boy that day.

James 5:16a is the key: "Therefore confess your sins to one another, and pray for one another, so that you may be healed."

Arlyne did the very same thing with Tim, but she spread their conversations over a period of a few months. Every time she would remember one of our former battles, she would ask Tim to forgive her for that episode.

Even to this day, if Tim believes he may have hurt us with something he said or did, he asks us to forgive him. This is a learned response.

Obviously, it will do no good to ask someone for forgiveness if you don't intend to work hard at changing your ways through the power of the Holy Spirit (Eph. 6:10-18). A child or teenager is always frustrated by a hypocritical parent who won't admit his or her mistakes and sins. If the hypocrite claims to be a Christian, the young person will often rebel against Christ as a direct result.

A Word to Wives

Never correct or argue with your husband in front of your kids. You are challenging authority in your children's minds when you do that. Later your kids will begin to do the same thing: attack authority. They will feel *they* can mouth off at you, then at teachers, police, even God. And Dad will be reduced to a wimp in their eyes, so his authority will be short-circuited too.

A Word to Husbands

Never correct or argue with your wife in front of your kids either. You are not a referee but a husband and father. If your child or teenager speaks rudely to his mother, you may feel your wife did something that caused the attack. But God commands you to be your wife's "protector" (1 Pet. 3:7).

Hopefully, one day your children will grow into marvelous husbands and wives. But they will struggle in those roles unless they had a good example to follow from you. When a kid loses respect for his parent's authority, he tends to lose all respect for *any* authority, including God.

Being Bitter Won't Make Things Better

God has given this caution to parents:

> See to it that no one comes short of the grace of God;
> that no root of bitterness springing up cause trouble, and
> by it many be defiled (Heb. 12:15).

Bitterness is one of Satan's most powerful weapons. It causes married couples and hurting single parents to lash out with their tongues at the one who did them wrong. A bitter statement may be true, but when a kid hears strong charges against the other parent, it can quickly defile the kid. Whether the kid voices it or not, he will believe he must be just like that awful parent. After all, he came from that person. The devil will make sure the kid feels defiled.

Never let your tongue go loose with accusations, hatred or demeaning comments about your kids' dad or mom, except in counseling with someone who knows the Lord intimately, cares about you and can help set you free. And *never* do it even under these circumstances with any of your kids present. Your words at such times can only defile (make sick or destroy emotionally) you and your kids. Here's what God says about it:

> Never pay back evil for evil to anyone. Respect what is right in the sight of all [mankind]. If possible, so far as it depends on you, be at peace with all [mankind]. Never take your own revenge, beloved, but leave room for the wrath of God, for it is written, "Vengeance is mine, I will repay," says the Lord.
>
> But if your enemy is hungry, feed him, and if he is thirsty, give him a drink; for in so doing you will heap burning coals upon his [or her] head. Do not be overcome with evil, but overcome evil with good (Rom. 12:17-21).

Don't Enter Into a State of Denial

This does not mean you should condone evil behavior or let it keep hurting you or your kids. "Peace at any price" is far too costly. Romans 12:18 says, "If possible be at peace with all men." Sometimes it isn't possible to keep the peace. James Dobson addresses this point in his remarkable book *Love Must Be Tough*. Sin in a husband or wife *always* needs to be confronted, or it will contaminate the whole family. But it is always possible to keep a Christ-centered attitude if you are centered on Christ.

The world thinks it has to scream loudly because it has no answers! But don't join them in the screaming. Christ is your answer.

Healthy family dialogue will hit pockets of disagreement sometimes. There is nothing wrong with that. Not everyone hangs toilet paper the same way. But you can lovingly agree to disagree, unless it's an issue clearly stated in the Bible.

The devil is an equal opportunity employer! He doesn't care whom he makes mad, as long as that person will stay mad. As nineteenth-century philosopher Robert Ingersoll said, "Anger blows out the candle of the mind!"

The first rule of Christian communication whenever you are

talking with anyone, but especially with your spouse or a member of your family, is Ephesians 4:15a: "Speak the truth in love."

> If you are angry, don't sin by nursing your grudge. Don't let the sun go down with you still angry — get over it quickly; for when you are angry you give a mighty foothold to the devil (Eph. 4:26-27, TLB).

Here's the prayer to keep in mind when you feel tempted to attack your spouse, or anyone else, verbally:

> Set a guard, O Lord, over my mouth; keep watch over the door of my lips (Ps. 141:3).

2. Needed for bonding: equal affection for all kids in your family.

Question: Why did Joseph's brothers want to kill him?

Answer: Because when parents play favorites, it's murder!

Comparison Is the Root of Inferiority

In spite of having several sons, Isaac doted on his son Joseph. All the rest of Isaac's sons felt far less loved. They decided Joseph should be killed. God rescued Joseph, eventually making him the second highest official in Egypt. But the emotional pain Joseph suffered on the way to Egyptian rulership was largely because of a father who didn't treat each of his kids equally.

One day when our son, David, was four and Beth was six, Arlyne was reading to them about Joseph and Mary going to "*Beth*lehem." David stopped Arlyne and asked, "Is there a *David*lehem?" In his young mind, if God named a city after his sister, He should also have named one after him! Happily, Arlyne was able to inform him that *Beth*lehem is the city of *David*. But a parent isn't always that lucky!

Some Kids Are Easy to Favor

It starts even with the nursery rhymes that tell little girls they are made of "sugar and spice and everything nice." But a boy is made of "snips and snails and puppy dog tails." It sounds like something Gloria Steinem would write!

Parents, grandparents or even neighbors and friends who make a fuss over the "cute" little girl or boy, ignoring the homelier one, often cause deep feelings of inferiority in the one ignored.

Some kids are easy to love — especially gifted children, teenagers with scholarship abilities, athletes who score all the touchdowns or the musicians who can entertain every visitor in your home. Such kids get rave reviews even from Uncle Snerdley but often become spoiled.

Meanwhile, those who are neglected slink away with hurt feelings of rejection. They may desperately try to succeed in some area to gain the missing attention of their parents. Or they may rebel out of the frustration of feeling a complete failure — and even get in trouble just to be recognized.

Parents who spend equal time with each of the children separately as well as together are parents who are bonding in an extremely healthy way. A mentally healthy child from that kind of home will be more easily introduced to Christ than either the favored, selfish one who fails to believe he needs God or the neglected child who may find it hard to believe Christ could ever love "unlovable" them.

Don't Give a Handicap to the Handicapped

The handicapped child too often gets one of two treatments: star billing or an exit visa. Both responses are equally damaging to every child or teenager in the family.

I had a great friend in college who had a brother with Down's Syndrome. Whenever I was at my friend's home, I watched the parents doting on that brother. Even though my friend got high grades, held student body offices, was paying his own way through college and continually tried to please his parents and brother, he received no praise from them. One day he just quit trying and turned to alcohol, which ultimately led to his untimely death.

His parents had made two mistakes. First, they mistakenly thought they were guilty for bringing this child into the world, and they were trying to make it up to their handicapped son. Second, rather than thanking God for their other son, praising him for his achievements and letting him know how glad they were to be his parents, they evidently thought this was unnecessary since he was normal. But they should have paid equal attention to both of their sons.

In far too many homes where handicapped kids live, the opposite situation is just as tragic. These homes shun or hide the handicapped child. Such children are left out of family pictures, told to stay out of the way when company comes, treated as if they didn't exist and spoken to with hateful words. This is a sinful way to deal with any human being, especially your own child. The handicapped need love, attention and a relationship with Jesus Christ just as everybody else does.

An actual list of high achievers among the handicapped would fill this book and many more besides. One of Arlyne and my closest friends is legally blind. From the beginning of her life her mother told her she could do anything she set her mind to do. She was told to "Go for it!" She did, does and will. We sometimes find it hard to keep up with her!

What do you do with a handicapped child? Thank God for your handicapped son or daughter. Take care of his or her needs as much as possible. Then do all you can to help your child overcome the handicap. Treat him or her equally with each of the other kids in your home. God views that child as a blessing. So should parents and siblings.

Even if the handicap is so severe it requires that your son or daughter be placed in a special, caring home or hospital — keep caring about your child and showing that you love him or her as one of your kids.

Oh, Baby!

Be certain you never let a new baby force other children in the home to become second-class citizens. Love the baby. Let everybody "oooh" and "aah" over it. But include the whole family in raising any new members. Talk with visitors about any positive things each of the other kids is doing. Let your friends know what a help it is to have your older ones with you.

Often tell the baby in front of the other kids how "blessed" he is to have such wonderful big brothers or sisters. Tell the older ones how important they are to the baby. Treat your kids *equally.*

Kids Don't Choose Their Gender

Please be assured: It is *God,* not kids, who determines whether they are born male or female:

> For Thou didst form my inward parts; Thou didst weave me in my mother's womb (Ps. 139:13).

Never tell a child that he or she is not the sex you wanted. *God* chose to give you either a boy or a girl. Never force a girl into culturally "masculine" activities (that is, football, boxing, heavy-duty physical sports). And don't force a boy to do culturally "female" activities (playing with dolls, knitting and the like). It doesn't make them more sensitive and understanding if you force this kind of behavior. You violate every rule of God if you do that.

This doesn't mean there is anything wrong with tomboys or with boys who, like football legend Rosey Grier, love to crochet. It just means that males are males and females are females. God made them that way. Let them be who they are.

> Train up a child in the way they should go, and in keeping with their individual gift or bent (Prov. 22:6, AMP).

Help your kids develop their "individual gift or bent"--their own interests and talents. You may be raising a male or female aviator or zoologist. As you help them discover more about their areas of interest, they will be more and more fulfilled and find real challenge and purpose in life, or they may change their areas of interest.

One of the silliest things anyone can do is to ask a pregnant woman, "What do you want, a boy or a girl?" The only wise answer is "Yes!"

Why Are Kids in a Family Often So Different?

Dr. Roger Sperry won the Nobel Prize in medicine and physiology in 1981 for discovering different brain functions in males and females. Between the sixteenth and twenty-sixth week of gestation a phenomenon occurs in boy babies about 80 percent of the time that does not occur in girl babies. Two chemicals are released that wash away at the *corpus callosum* (the connecting fibers between the left side of the brain and the right side). This leaves these boy babies (nearly all are right-handed) left-brain dominant from the womb on. Girls (and most left-handed males) do not have this physical experience. Thus females (and most left-handed males) are bilateral thinkers.

This phenomenon affects everything from a memory for details (most wives can tell you the colors used at their wedding no matter how long ago it took place — most husbands can't remember the color of their wives' eyes!) to the fact that most women are very relational or people-oriented. Men tend to be more "thing-oriented" — they are far more interested in fishing poles, footballs and television sets.

Artistic and musical talent tends to come from the right side of the brain. Eighty-five percent of male world-class artists and musicians are left-handed!

In spite of different brain functions, it probably can't be stressed enough that every kid is unique and an important *individual* in God's plan. Parents who understand this and raise each of their kids with real love and discipline nearly always raise kids who are a plus.

3. Needed for bonding: honest parents

> Do not lie to one another, since you laid aside the old
> self with its evil practice (Col. 3:9).

Parents who keep their promises have children who grow up to be trusting adults. But parents who are careless about making promises or don't keep their word raise pessimists who are deeply suspicious of others and have difficulty trusting God and His Word.

Never Lie to a Child

A lie, to a child, is *anything untrue.*

Words children five and under usually interpret as meaning absolutely "yes!" include: *probably, perhaps* and *maybe.* Even older children will usually think you've confirmed something with these words.

Never Teach Your Children to Lie

I was at a church leader's home when I heard his wife shout from the kitchen, "Tell that person on the telephone I'm not home!" It hurt to hear those words. The obedient child did just what Mommy had told her to do. But I wondered how long it would be before that child did the same thing to Mommy or Daddy.

The Bible says:

> Simply let your "Yes" be "Yes," and your "No," "No"; anything beyond this comes from the evil one (Matt. 5:37, NIV).

If your kids know you lie or go back on your word, you are training them up in the way they will almost certainly go. Certainly not God's way, because

> Satan is the father of lies (John 8:44).

One Thursday when our kids were young our whole family was listening to Vin Scully announce a Dodger baseball game over the radio. The Dodgers won in the ninth inning. I enthusiastically shouted, "Let's go see them play at Dodger Stadium tomorrow night!" The kids let out a whoop of delight.

An hour later Arlyne and I were alone in the kitchen when she put her arms around me and said, "Honey, have you forgotten how early your airplane leaves Saturday morning?" I groaned. I had forgotten the early flight I'd have to take to New York for a special meeting that night. But I'd given my word.

The Dodgers won again that Friday night, and my whole family and I were there in the stands loaded with hot dogs, peanuts and popcorn. We had a ball. The next morning Arlyne and the kids woke up when I did and lined up to kiss me good-bye. When David kissed me, he said, "Thanks for keeping your word about the ball game, Dad!" Somehow, even as quietly as she'd spoken it to me, David had overheard Arlyne's word about the airplane. He knew I'd made a tough decision. But, without my knowing until then, he'd also learned one more time that he could count on his dad to keep his word.

If I ever forgot a promise I'd made to one of the kids, Arlyne, like the Holy Spirit, would "come alongside" me with a loving reminder. She always did it away from the kids so that I wouldn't be embarrassed. But we both know how important our promises are. We claim to be Christians, and God always keeps His Word to us.

Soon your children will follow your example instead of your advice!

Dear Ray:

You must hear more marriage complaints than a bartender does. Well, until not too long ago, my bartender was the one who got them all from me. Now I've been a Christian for two years and married for too long. Too bad my wife and I aren't boxers. We could make money in a ring. We do plan to come to your seminar in Kailua-Kona, Hawaii. If the marriage doesn't work out, maybe I can find somebody in a grass skirt! Also, how do I get close to my teenage son? I honestly don't know how. I'll see you soon.

Aloha!

Turn the hearts of the fathers
back to the children, and the
disobedient to the attitude
of the righteous, so as to make
a people prepared for the Lord.
Luke 1:17b

SEVEN

BONDING, AND I DON'T MEAN JAMES!

*Too often an abandoned
child is one still living
with its parents.*

WE'RE ONLY GETTING started with the things your kids deeply need from you as their parent. Let's review:

1. Don't fight.

2. Treat all your kids equally.

3. Never lie to your kids.

As a parent, make these rules absolutes in the way you live with your kids.

135

In this chapter and the next we will continue to explore the need for bonding with your children. As you meet these needs, the devil will lose territory with your kids and your home.

4. Needed for bonding: parents who obviously love each other.

President John F. Kennedy thrilled America with his prediction that we would put man on the moon in ten years. As a nation we got so excited about it that we did it in eight years. That is the power of agreement and togetherness.

President Lyndon Johnson got so discouraged he declined to run for a second term. Why? Because he felt greatly responsible for our nation's disagreement and division over the war in Vietnam.

Agreement in Christ with each other and togetherness in decision making will keep a husband and wife in a strong position of leadership within their family. But disagreement and division between parents is all a kid needs to play one against the other until both give up and let the kid take over and control them both.

> Husbands, love your wives, just as Christ also loved the church and gave Himself up for her (Eph. 5:25).
>
> Encourage the young women to love their husbands (Titus 2:4a).

Hug and kiss in front of your kids. Of course, there are limits! But there isn't a kid in this world who doesn't want and need to have Mom and Dad love each other. I grieve for any child who doesn't regularly see his parents touch lovingly. One of the saddest results of growing up in an unaffectionate home is that the children often grow up to be unaffectionate adults as well. In some homes you wonder how the parents ever had any kids! Never let it be that way at your home.

Ping-Pong Kids

Hundreds of teenagers have told me, "I wouldn't even care if my parents loved *me* if they just loved each other." They don't really mean they wouldn't need their parents' love, but they are being torn apart emotionally by the turmoil in their home.

Kids nearly always love both their parents or very much want to be able to love them. But when they are forced to choose between their parents in the name of "loyalty" to one or the other, they don't do it well. The pain inside their broken hearts stays too intense.

One kid who had been apprehended by the police for shoplifting told me, "I feel like a ping-pong ball. My folks are split up. I'm supposed to spend half the time with my dad and half the time with my mom. Dad keeps cussing out Mom. He gets drunk and sleeps with other women. My mom plays the martyr. She goes to church, but she doesn't live the life. She cries a lot and doesn't cuss, but her words hurt just as much. I can't stand it. I was supposed to be going to my dad's today, but I jumped off the bus when it stopped in this city. I was stealing enough to buy me some food. Now I guess they'll feed me and let me sleep here in this jail."

A teenage girl said, "Yes, I sleep with guys. Before we sleep together they tell me they love me. I like that. I never hear it from my folks. They're too busy screaming at each other to stop and say they love me. Besides, the hate they both show all the time proves they don't even know what love is."

Samson was asleep when he lost his strength. So are a lot of parents.

The total healing of a marriage may seem to take a long time (Luke 18:1) But please take it from a couple who has a healed marriage, Arlyne and me: The walk and wait of being healed is worth what it takes to get there.

> At all times [you] ought to pray and not lose heart (Luke 18:1b).
>
> For if you forgive men for their transgressions, your heavenly Father will also forgive you. But if you do not forgive men, then your Father will not forgive your transgressions (Matt. 6:14-15).

Your kids are worth staying together as parents. And they deserve a happy couple as their parents. Not a perfect couple, but a couple working at God's perfect plans for them and their family.

There have been far too many moments when even as a Christian I would like to have had a chiropractor get my foot out of my mouth! I've had to apologize too many times in my life. We Christians always have to apologize when we've blown it with words or dumb actions. The words of the apostle Paul have inspired me at all such times. After saying that he wasn't "perfect" yet, Paul said:

> Forgetting what lies behind and reaching forward to

what lies ahead, I press on toward the goal for the prize
of the upward call of God in Christ Jesus (Phil. 3:13b-14).

A word to those who haven't received an apology yet: The
happiest married person is often a person with a poor memory!

Years ago I read of a woman who, at her bridal shower, told her
friends, "I am writing down ten things, and I've already told my
husband-to-be that if he ever does any of these things I will divorce
him!" At her golden wedding anniversary some of her friends reminded
her of that statement and asked her to share what ten things she had
written down. She said, "Well, I never did get around to writing
anything down. But every time my husband does anything that upsets
me, I just tell him, 'You'd better be glad *that's* not one of the ten!'"

Our Own Moms and Dads

Kids who grow to adulthood with both parents do far better in
their own marriages and with life choices than those who come
from broken homes.

My own dad and mom weren't always happy campers. Dad was
thirteen years older than Mom and a workaholic. In order to
provide for our family he worked in the nursery that he owned
from sunup until long after sundown, seven days a week. When he
wasn't serving customers, he was watering plants. He was a volun-
teer fireman, an active Rotarian and tired nearly all the time.

Mom tried to cope under the circumstances. She was expected to
work alongside Dad and keep the home going as if she were not
working outside it. She worried about my needs a lot more than my
busy dad did, so they argued a lot. I sometimes wondered if they might
divorce. But it never happened. They made it. In fact, the last
several years after Dad semi-retired were their happiest together.

What did that do for me? So much. During the dark days of my
own marriage I realized that if my folks could stick it out, so could
I. God used my folks as part of the Superglue to hold me in my
marriage. In spite of their problems, how I thank God for the
example Mom and Dad set for me.

Arlyne thought "Christian marriages" always stayed together. In her
mind divorce was not an option. Her parents were Christians. In 1994
they celebrated their fifty-ninth wedding anniversary. They made great
role models for her. How thankful we are for that heritage.

What If My Spouse Is Committed to Sin?

Some marriages grieve the Holy Spirit (Eph. 4:30). Mine did for many years. Sin always does. That's one of the reasons why God commands every single person:

Do not be unequally yoked with unbelievers (2 Cor. 6:14a, KJV).

And then He goes on to ask:

What has a believer in common with an unbeliever? (1 Cor. 6:15b, KJV).

A single person who claims to be a Christian but dates an unbeliever is denying his or her own Christianity. After all, if Christ is really that person's Lord and best friend, would they date their best friend's *worst* enemy? Of course not.

The single Christian marrying an unbeliever is headed for torment from the devil himself. I have seen thousands of unbelievers come to Christ in my seminars. But I have never seen it happen without a hideous amount of emotional pain in the marriage first. "The wages of sin is death" (Rom. 6:23a), and that often includes death to happiness, peace, safety — even the spiritual death of kids, just as Cain died spiritually after his parents disobeyed God.

Often one of the spouses is born again *after* a couple marries. Suddenly the sins they shared are no longer appreciated or desired by the Christian. The unsaved spouse grows angrier. Friction can turn to all-out war in such a marriage. The children are torn between their parents. They will most likely also be torn between righteousness and unrighteousness. Younger children may be more easily persuaded to choose Christ. But a teenager already sold out to a lost lifestyle may want the Christian parent to "hang it on their beak!"

If your situation is like either of these homes, here are some questions to ponder:

1. How safe are you if you remain with your spouse? Are you or your kids apt to be physically harmed if you don't separate?

2. Does your spouse show any signs of repentance? Or is he (or she) adamantly defending his sin?

3. Are your children being persuaded to enter into your spouse's lifestyle of blatant sin? Or are they using your spouse's sin to defend their own?

4. Have you prayed diligently? (Luke 18:1).

5. Do you have a Christ-centered prayer partner of your same gender?

6. Have you received godly Christian counsel?

7. Are you being taught and fellowshipping in a Bible-believing, Christ-centered church?

8. What is the Holy Spirit telling you to do?

Honestly answer all of the above questions. Then do as the Holy Spirit directs you. It may be best to take your children and separate. Either leave or get a court order and have your spouse leave.

Separation Is Not Divorce

> But to the married I give instructions, not I, but the Lord, that the wife should not leave her husband (but if she does leave, let her remain unmarried, or else be reconciled to her husband), and that the husband should not send his wife away (1 Cor. 7:10-11).

Separation for the protection of life or limb of any member of a family and for the purpose of waking a sinning spouse to his or her need for full repentance is often wisdom blessed by God. Separation is not divorce. It is space given for the Holy Spirit to accomplish what only He can do. The sinner will still have the free will to reject even the Holy Spirit. Often temporary separation is all that is needed to show the sinner that his or her spouse and Christ will not let him continue in the destructive lifestyle. If you are caught in a situation where such action may be necessary, prayerfully read James Dobson's book *Love Must Be Tough* and follow the leading of the Holy Spirit.

Remember: Empty threats are as valuable as an empty can of beans to a starving man. Don't say what you don't mean. The rule of communication, no matter how intense, must always be Ephesians 4:15: "Speaking the truth in love."

You Can Still Have a Marriage Plus

Consider the following letter written to me one year after this wife attended a Marriage Plus Love-In at a church in Pennsylvania.

Dear Ray:

Black eyes, broken nose, arm in a cast and hating my husband, we came to your Love-In. He sat in one section of the church, while I sat in another. We were separated by court order, and if he had as much as said hello I would have had him arrested. Yet by the end of one week I went to him and knew I was talking to a brand-new man.

The first night of your seminar he gave his life to Christ and meant it. I kept my distance but prayed, forgiving my husband for the hell he'd given our kids and me for six years. I still didn't think there was any hope for reconciliation.

You taught the Bible like I'd never heard before that whole week. Tons of pain vanished while I listened. My husband wasn't the only one forever changed. So was I.

I raised my hand that final night, letting you know I was cancelling my divorce plans. My husband and I talked, soon started "dating" each other again by double-dating, and this Christian husband of mine moved back into our home three months ago. We're in church all the time now and love it. We love each other a whole lot, and the kids have responded powerfully to the transformation in their dad.

One thing more: He has said on several occasions that he never would have gone to your seminar if I hadn't gotten that court order and legally driven him out of the house. That woke him up. He knew something had to change. You taught him *how* to change.

Thanks, Ray, from the bottom of my family's heart.

Sin must be confronted. Allowed to continue, it is like a cancer — it will spread. Your kids must be protected from incest, homosexuality, adultery, violence or the attraction to an addictive sin of any kind. These types of sins are all addressed by one Greek word, *porneia*, which means "a spirit of whoredom." *Porneia* is translated in

Matthew 5:32 and Matthew 19:9 into the English words *unchastity, fornication, adultery* and so forth, depending on which Bible translation you use. Whoredom (sexual addiction) is hideous. The Lord twice said *porneia* is the *exception* that would even allow for divorce if a sinning spouse refuses to stop his or her sin. Your kids need to be protected from the devil himself.

What to Do Until God Comes Through

There are wife beaters and husband beaters. Both must be stopped. If you would like to discuss your situation with an outstanding counselor on domestic violence, phone my friend Marilyn Post at the Domestic Violence Research Center in Quincey, Illinois — (217) 222-3711. Tell her I told you to call. She'll help you.

If you are hurting in your marriage, or your kids are hurting because of what is happening in your home, please call (206) 848-6400 and get a list of our upcoming seminars. Ask your spouse to attend a seminar with you. There is a far better answer than divorce.

Now You Get to See My Snapshots!

What do you think when someone talks about his wife and kids, reaches for his wallet and says, "I just happen to have some pictures here." If you are like most people you'll hurriedly look at the pictures and say appropriate things like, "Wow! Isn't Elmira cute! And this grandson of yours is named 'Doodles'? Hmmm."

Well, I just happen to have some word pictures here in which I plan to show you my kids, but I'm giving you fair warning. If you need to mow the lawn, bathe the dog or paint your house, and you'd rather get it done now, I'll understand — maybe!

First let me tell you why I want you to see my kids. They're all adults now, but they were once very normal kids in a house like yours. We lived through twelve years with a dachshund named Rinkles and the last fifteen years with a cockapoo named Taffy. For many years we lived in the same house. But there was one major difference between your home and mine. It is very probable that both you and your spouse lived in your house with your kids. Arlyne did live there. But I have traveled often nonstop for the past twenty-four years. Yes, there were very special seasons of time when I was at home and extended times when the whole family traveled together. But most of every year I have been away more weeks than I have been home.

How did our love survive? How did my kids adapt? Well, we thank God for Ma Bell. I've reached out and touched every "some-one" at my house as often as I've been away. I've counseled, prayed, read to, cheered for and shared my life with each of them — and most of all with my wife — nightly. And praise the Lord for fax machines. Since their invention I've been a daily customer when overseas. Servicemen and women, traveling salespeople, evangelists, athletes and traveling pastors can have great marriages even though they travel regularly. I do.

But What If Junior Cries?

This brings up the oft-heard comment from a mother who is wean-ing herself very reluctantly from her baby, "I *can't* go out with my husband tonight and leave a baby-sitter with my child. He'll cry!"

In my early years as a Bible teacher, when I'd be leaving for a month, six-year-old Tim would stand at the door crying, "Daddy, don't go! Come back! Pleeeze!" It would rip my heart out. But I went with God's promise from the Gospel of Mark:

> Jesus said, "Truly I say to you, there is no one who has left house or brothers or sisters or mother or father or children or farms, for My sake and for the gospel's sake, but that he shall receive a hundred times as much now in the present age, houses and brothers and sisters and mothers and children and farms, along with persecutions; and in the world to come, eternal life" (Mark 10:29-30).

God has kept that promise (even the part about persecutions)! One night in 1977, while my family and I were living in Blenheim, New Zealand, Tim and I were doing the dishes. (Arlyne was in another city teaching at a women's retreat.) Tim said to me, "Dad, why don't you write down everything you teach? And then when I'm a little older, I can go out and teach it too. That way we can get the world won to Christ twice as fast!"

Because of a bonding between Tim and me, in person and by phone, he grew up wanting to please both his earthly father and his heavenly Father. Each of our kids has done the same.

143

Tim was close to turning three when he prayed with Arlyne on our living room couch, asking Jesus Christ into his heart. Elizabeth was with us at a church meeting where one of our visiting evangelist friends was ministering. As he gave the altar call, she went forward at the age of four.

We were a bit worried about our youngest, David. We feared he might be our family heathen! It wasn't until he was five that he made his trip to the altar.

Each of our kids remembers their conversion very clearly. All three of them had made "false starts" even before their real born-again experience. But each of them looks to the time I've just described as the moment they accepted Jesus Christ as Savior and Lord.

Did we push them into these decisions? No. Each made them because of what they had heard through Bible stories, songs, prayers and Sunday school and what they had seen of Christ in other people's lives.

Did we see huge changes in them as soon as they were born again? Not really. They were very young and hadn't messed their lives up with anything more than cookies and milk. We're so thankful. God does answer prayer.

Our kids were very normal kids. I wouldn't know so much about effective discipline if Arlyne and I had never needed to use it! But we have often seen the love, tenderness, caring and right decision making in each of their lives because they did (and still do) love the Lord.

In fact, we were surprised one afternoon when Elizabeth was ten to hear her evict a neighbor boy from our house. She told him, "If you are going to swear, go home! Come back again only when your mouth is clean." The boy went home and eagerly came back later with his "clean mouth."

Although all three of our kids went to Christian elementary school, they were ready for the challenge of living for Christ without compromise by the time they started public high school. Their closest friends were committed Christians too. They knew how to have far more fun than those who had to throw up after a night of wild partying.

They all spent at least one full summer in their high school years on overseas missions trips with other teenagers. They all attended (David still is) Christian colleges. All are in (or headed for) full-time ministry in their careers. They believe marriage and parenting are higher callings than any other form of ministry. But if a man or woman does not know how to take care of their own family, how can they take care of the church of God? (see 1 Tim. 3:5).

It hasn't been easy. There have been times of great pain. I wasn't there to see Tim ordained to the ministry. Elizabeth sang a solo with her youth choir at the Church on the Way, and I missed it. I was also gone when David won a first-place trophy with his drama team in competition with the entire Los Angeles high school district.

Elizabeth may have felt my absence from home the hardest. During puberty she would often break down crying because she missed her daddy. Many times I suggested to Arlyne and the kids that I enter some other form of work or ministry that would allow me to stay home. But Arlyne and the kids believe, as I do, that God has sent me out to set families free, and we have been in this ministry together.

So going out for an evening and leaving your children home with a Christian baby-sitter won't hurt them emotionally, even if they cry. Just spend special time with them when you are home. What they will learn is that Mom loves Dad and vice versa.

Real Communication Is Essential for Bonding

Daily communication is essential for a happy Christian home. Your kids need to know they can talk with you at any time. The last thing I would tell my kids before leaving on a ministry trip was, "Anytime you need me, phone me." My hotel phone number always sits right beside the telephone at home.

One day Tim phoned me while we were in New Zealand — we were a thousand miles apart from each other. That call was very expensive — but urgent. He phoned to ask if he could have a white rat!

My Darlin' Arlyne

Arlyne has made a quality difference in my years of ministry. Many times I have spoken of this traveling life for ministry as "a strange way to live." She always corrects me by saying, "This ministry isn't strange. It is unique and full of challenge and adventure." That kind of input has given our kids peace and motivation rather than self-pity, bitterness or resentment toward God or me.

One day in the not-too-distant future each of our kids will join

Arlyne and me in heaven. The multitudes that have been affected eternally because of their willingness and partnership in giving their dad to Christ's ministry will be well worth any pain we have suffered for it here.

5. *Needed for bonding: great fun and fellowship between parents and kids.*

The family that plays together and prays together stays together. Jesus said:

> The thief comes only to steal and kill, and destroy; I came that they might have life, and might have it abundantly (John 10:10).

Jesus came to bring life. Some Christians work so many hours they don't have time to experience life.

The average American father spends less than twelve minutes of good interaction with his children a week.[1] The average Dad spends thirty-seven seconds a day holding and talking to his baby before it can talk.[2] Yet if a baby isn't cuddled and spoken to between birth and the age of two, it's almost certain to grow up sick and unaffectionate.

Teenagers are often afraid of hugs. They may think it makes them look like a child and that they are "too old" for hugging. Slip your arms around them anyway and let them know you care. A kiss on the cheek for both your sons and daughters is great. There is no age at which love and open affection aren't healthy.

Children Spell "Love" Differently

Children spell love T-I-M-E. So if you're trying to figure out what to spend on your kids, spend *time!*

One day when Tim was six, I was sitting at my desk looking over voting materials. Tim walked up to me with a baseball cap on his head and a bat slung over his shoulder. He asked me, "What are you doing, Daddy?"

I told him, "Son, I'm trying to figure out how I'm going to vote in this next election."

"Can I do it too?" he asked.

"No," I responded laughingly. "This is for older people. There'll come a time when you'll be old enough."

Tim looked straight into my eyes and said, "You know, *older* people just care about other *older* people. Jesus — He cares about us *little* people too. Would you go out and play baseball with me?"

I got up, went out and played baseball with him! Romans 8:29 says I'm to be just like Jesus, and that's exactly what Jesus would have done!

That six-year-old is happily married now with two beautiful children of his own. Listen: If you've got the idea that you'll work seven days a week, eighteen hours a day *now*, and then one day soon you'll have more time for your kids — you are only fooling yourself.

Things can never substitute for love. Money or presents *can't* replace dads and moms. The work will wait while you show the child the rainbow. But the rainbow won't wait while you do the work!

Go places with your family — picnics, fishing, to sporting events and school functions. Play Monopoly, Scrabble, Clue and other kinds of fun family games. If you as a parent don't like these kinds of games, like your kids enough to play them anyway.

Along with group activities as a family, do individual things with each kid. Write these dates on the calendar at least a week ahead and never overlook them. Throwing a ball for an hour at a park, bicycling, playing miniature golf, shooting hoops, making homemade ice cream together for the rest of the family, fishing or hiking are all great "together" experiences with just one of your kids at a time.

By the time a child is two they should be putting away their toys when they've finished playing with them. Let them "help you" do simple household jobs. Expect mistakes but encourage them to continue. And let them know you appreciate what they do.

Keep increasing the assignments as they become old enough to handle them. Mix work with play. A few hours on a garden project or building something can set all kinds of good training in motion. It can create fellowship, accomplishment and fun.

The parent has to be patient and allow the child to make mistakes without a stern or sarcastic lecture, or taking the job away from the child. If your child or teenager is made to feel like a failure it will spoil any adventure together and destroy a trusting relationship.

The Ugly Duckling Who Turned Into a Swan

My daughter, Elizabeth, had a rough time at puberty. Most kids do. In fact, any young person between the ages of eleven and fifteen who *likes himself* is a living miracle! Most young people between these ages think they're the ugliest thing that was ever coughed up on a beach!

Because I knew my daughter was going through such emotional pain, I made a special date with her. First, though, I had Arlyne pick her up after school, and they went shopping for a new dress. Then she went to the beauty shop for a new hairdo. By now she was glowing! Meanwhile I left my office early and stopped by the florist to buy a corsage for her. I'd saved up a bit of money for that night and took her to a very fancy restaurant. She felt like the belle of the ball. She knew she was lovely. The puberty blues began to fade.

A Note of Caution in a Sick Society

In today's troubled society I suppose I should add a postscript to the above story. Tragically, incest is on the rapid increase in America. The average victim of incest is seven years old. This chapter is on bonding. Any healthy parent-child relationship will nearly always be destroyed forever by even one incident of incest or sexual abuse with any kid.

A few years ago *U.S. News & World Report* reported that about 70 percent of adolescent drug addicts were involved in some form of sexual abuse. Approximately 75 percent of adolescent prostitutes had been involved in incestuous relationships. Since that time sexual abuse has become one of the three major reasons why children run away from home.

May God protect our families!

Young people tend to accept your ideas if they accept you. And they tend to reject your ideas and philosophies — and your God — if they reject you.

Live so that when people tell your son
he reminds them of you, he will stick
out his chest — not his tongue!

Dear Ray:

My kids have more friends than they can count. (And I don't think some of their friends *do* count!) I'm about to put a "Quaran-*teen*ed" sign on our front door just to keep the brats away.

What worries me most is that my daughter is almost ready to date. She's fourteen and thinks she's thirty-four. Do I even dare to think there might be rules she should keep? How could I possibly get them across to her?

One more thing: How can we get our kids to close the genera-tion gap between them and my wife and me? Maybe we haven't been doing everything right.

Sad Dad

But you shall receive power
when the Holy Spirit has come
upon you; and you shall
be My witnesses.
Acts 1:8a

EIGHT

BONDS HAVE MORE FUN!

*Yelling at kids is not
the way to make
the home a
howling success!*

THE POSTER READS: "Buy Bonds. It Will Keep America Strong."
Let me change the wording to something even more important:
"Bond With Your Kids. It Will Keep America Even Stronger."
We have seen five essential commandments for bonding that
will meet your kids' needs and fulfill you as a parent:

1. Don't fight.
2. Treat all your kids equally.
3. Never lie to your kids.

4. Be parents who obviously love each other.

5. Work to keep an atmosphere of fun and fellowship between you and your kids.

We'll find two more essential bonding rules in this chapter.

6. Needed for bonding: Treat all your kids' friends as welcome visitors in your house.

I can just see a father reading that and thinking, What? Has Ray gone mad? He couldn't know the little monsters that my kids have as friends. If he did, he wouldn't make such a foolish suggestion!

But as a Christian parent who cares about your family, think about this particular point of bonding.

If you have little monsters in your neighborhood, start a Christian club for kids. Not the kind of club with which you whack heads — that would be *un*-Christian! — but a club that is Christ-centered and biblical. Use Christian videos, Bible stories and games, and "un-monster" the neighborhood! Talk with your pastor about this, and reread the suggestions given in chapter 5.

How close are you to people who either don't like your friends or speak negatively about them? Do their remarks about your friends draw you closer or push you further away? In the same way, if you are cold toward your kids' friends or speak against them, your kids are going to think you don't care much about them either.

Happy Kids Grow Up to Have Happy Kids

How you were treated as a child will often determine how you treat your children. If you are unable to have honest, close relationships with others, you need the healing of Christ. Seek God's help. He can set you free from the pain of the past. Christ came to set the captives free (Luke 4:18).

When our family moved to Chatsworth, California, in 1974, we knew no one in our neighborhood. But there were lots of kids living on our block. From the first day I decided to wave at each one as I drove down our street, whether I knew them or not. Soon it was like a parade whenever I drove by — everyone waved. Not long ago Arlyne and I moved to Washington, and the first day down our new street I began again. I think I've created a permanent wave!

Put Out the Welcome Mat

When your kids bring their friends around, even the ones you see often, stop whatever you're doing and chat with them for a moment. Make them feel welcome. Don't give these visitors the third degree or get too personal. Just let them know you care about them.

Few things give you more points with your own kids than to have their friends tell them, "You've got a great dad and mom." You couldn't buy that kind of good publicity with the best billboard in town!

This Goes for Teenagers Too

Teenagers are under extreme peer pressure. They really need to feel accepted by their friends. They want to be proud of their parents. They bring their friends home to see how fabulous their parents are (whether they tell you this or not). Friendly parents are rare — they stand out like jewels. It is one of the best forms of witnessing.

If, on the other hand, kids sense unkindness or a lack of enthusiastic response from their parents toward their friends, they deflate worse than a balloon and often get defensive.

Remember: Your teens are generally proud of their friends. Even if you see a terrible flaw in one of them, be careful how you share that news with your kids. If they feel you are attacking any of their friends, they may feel the need to stick up for them, even when they know you may be right. Ephesians 4:15 tells us to "speak the truth in love." Think of how you dislike hearing bad news about any of *your* friends.

Keeping That Testimony

Parents, be on guard against losing your testimony by what you *say* or *do* with your son or daughter or their friends. Never make jokes with your teenager's friend, saying things like, "I'd sure like a date with you!" Don't talk about their sexual attractiveness. Never make "off-color" comments. If a joke is doubtful, it's dirty. Dads, don't try to be "one of the boys." You are to be a man of God. Moms, you are to be a woman of God. You are His representative to these kids.

And there must be no filthiness and silly talk, or coarse jesting, which are not fitting (Eph. 5:4).

153

Your testimony is never going to be believed if you talk or act like the devil!

If you keep the respect of young people, it won't be surprising to find yourself leading some of them to Christ *without* preaching, because they will see Christ in you.

If you don't become involved with helping your kids select friends, expect the opposite. Retired Los Angeles Police Department assistant chief Robert Vernon says the most common reason teenagers give for breaking the law is: "I thought I'd lose all my friends unless I went along with what they were doing."

> A mirror reflects a man's face. But what he is really like is shown by the kind of friends he chooses (Prov. 27:19, TLB).

Help your kids choose good friends. Your kids' closest friends should always be Christians — so should yours (2 Cor. 6:14–7:1).

When your child or teenager has an opportunity to get together with other Christians, go out of your way to make it possible, even if it is inconvenient. The rewards and results will be worth it. Your child needs good friendships.

Staying Overnight

Know where your kids are — no matter how old — as long as you are responsible for them. Teach them to use the telephone to contact you if their plans change. Be equally thoughtful to them when you are away from home. They need to know you care.

If they haven't already, your children will reach an age when they will ask if they can stay overnight at a friend's house. Before you say yes, be sure they are old enough and fully aware of what body parts should never be touched by anyone. Be sure they would tell you if such a thing happened. But also tell them how great a sin it would be if they ever made up a story about someone doing that if they hadn't.

Know and approve of your child's friend and of his or her parents. Be sure your child has really been invited by the parents and that the parents will be home the entire time. Phone the parents first.

"But," you may say, "won't my kids be embarrassed if I do that? They'll think I'm with the FBI!"

Your kids won't mind if you do a subtle job of checking out the situation. When you phone, say, "Hi. This is _____. I just phoned to thank you for inviting my son [or daughter] over to your house for the night."

Chances are you'll hear, "Oh, we're delighted to have your child." But if you hear something like, "*Your* child? *Our* house? All night? *Tonight*?" then you'll know you have some further checking to do!

Sometimes it is a lot easier to have all "overnights" at *your* house. (Then buy some earplugs so you'll get your zzz's!)

7. Needed for bonding: Always answer your kids' questions.

Kids, like spouses, believe you care about them only if you listen to them. When they ask you a question, they need an answer. Caution: Be sure you know exactly what your child or teenager is asking.

Did you hear about little Johnny? He came into the house one day and asked his mother, "Mommy, where did I come from?"

Johnny's mother was flustered. She thought, Oh, oh! This is it — the sex lecture! So she got out her books, her charts and her colored slides.

Two hours later Johnny's mother turned to him and asked, "Now, son, do you understand where you came from?"

Little Johnny was sitting there bug-eyed. He looked at his mom and said, "Yeah. Billy, he just came from Pittsburgh. But me — wow!"

You Are Your Child's First Impression of God

"But if any of you lacks wisdom, let him ask of God, who gives to all [humans] generously and without reproach, and it will be given to him [or her]" (James 1:5, brackets added).

What greater honor could God have given you than to trust you as the interpreter of life to your child? You — especially dads — represent God to your family. Don't be annoyed when your children ask impossible questions. Be thankful they think you might know the answers! Get ready for some big questions.

What If They Ask About Dirty Words?

Prepare children when they are just learning to communicate by telling them, "If you hear a word and don't know what it means, come and ask me. I'll tell you. Sometimes people say words that are naughty, and I know you wouldn't want to say words like that."

At some point nearly every child is going to ask what some dirty word means. Take time to communicate. You'll seldom need to go into any graphic detail with very young children. But the older ones will need it spelled out for them. Certain sexually explicit words or terms will need definition. Always tell a child such words are not to be used in daily conversation. Let them know that sex words describe actions that God says are only to be used by a husband and wife.

Don't be fearful or over-wordy when you talk intimately with your kids. But don't be crude or casual about the subject either. Relax! Don't overreact. Use a low-key, matter-of-fact approach. God invented sex, so it is not dirty when it is being explained in a marriage context. Reassure your child that he hasn't done anything wrong by asking you the question.

As you establish this accepting, nonjudgmental relationship, your kids will become used to asking you about words and questionable behavior. Take all the time needed to communicate. (One of the finest helps in answering such questions is a series of books on sex, designed for each age level, published by Concordia Press. It is available at your local Christian bookstore.)

An Open Invitation to a Private Audience

Let your kids know they can come and talk privately with you about anything. After you hear what they are saying, express your thoughts without losing your temper or putting them down. Children who find that a parent is a thundering volcano or a screaming, weeping, bundle of nerves learn not to come to that parent with problems. The parent(s) who gets upset when things go wrong ends up cut off from his or her kids.

Keep from ending the communication by giving answers too quickly. Listen to their hearts. Quick answers or quickly reciting a Scripture verse may help you feel "right" and in charge of things. Your kids may even nod and stop talking (they know better than to argue with God). But they may not really agree with you or God. Discover their real feelings. Don't cut them off.

It's healthy to admit, "I've been through some of those same feelings." After warm communication and without preaching, let them know why God's way is the best way. Lead them to carry the thought to its probable conclusion, noting what a disaster an unbiblical conclusion could be.

Don't Get on a Soapbox

Every human has personal dislikes. One of mine is gum chewing. I do not chew gum, nor do I like watching others chew it. Gum chewing seems to me to be the nervous habit of people who hardly ever keep their mouths closed. These chewers make themselves totally unattractive. They make extremely irritating noises even when they don't pop their gum, and most resemble a cow chewing its cud.

Also, there is no polite way to park gum once a person ungracefully spits it from his or her mouth. After all, how can anyone *spit* gracefully? Chewed gum is hard to remove from a wastebasket; it is disgusting under a table; and it is nearly impossible to get off my shoe when I step on it. Finally, I have read excellent studies proving that chewing gum is harmful to a person's teeth and stomach. I hate gum! I believe the devil invented gum.

Now, if you are a gum chewer, how do you feel? That's exactly how kids feel when their parents get on a soapbox and preach at them over any nonbiblically condemned subject!

What About Fads?

When I was in elementary school I had a pair of glow-in-the-dark socks. They were "real gone" (which meant "cool" in those days). I wouldn't wear them today. Fads have a way of blowing in and blowing out just as quickly. Remember hula hoops?

You probably followed certain fads or did unusual things your mom and dad didn't appreciate. (For a long time David liked catsup on his pancakes!) If your son wants an earring in his ear or your daughter wants one in her nose, don't overreact — talk quietly with him or her. Express yourself without using cutting remarks. Speak what you believe to be the truth "in love" (Eph. 4:15). You'll most often see them accept your way of thinking because they know you have their best interests at heart.

On the other hand, if your teenager doesn't understand what is wrong with an activity, fashion or attitude that you oppose strongly, they may feel you are just being a grouch. Discuss your feelings, explaining both God's and your point of view. Do it calmly, yet with authority. If you and your teenager communicate comfortably, he or she will most likely respect your views, and you will probably be able to lead your teen to a decision both of you can accept.

Examples, Please

The Jesus movement of the 1970s was a magnificent time of seeing young people (and some not so young) from every corner of America come together in Jesus' name. These radical saints boldly spoke out for Christ in stark contrast to the drug culture and antiwar protestors of their generation. Millions of people were born again as a direct result. Yet many of the people whose lives were transformed by Christ hung on to their long hair and sandals.

Dignified members of traditional churches were challenged by those radical young people. Traditionalists didn't want hippies in their fresh, clean pews. Many cried out to their pastors, "Long hair is for women — either *they* go, *we* go or *you* go!"

It must never have crossed the minds of many of these well-meaning churchgoers that Jesus Christ probably looked more like the hippies than like them during the time God sent Him to earth. John the Baptist would have caused a church split with his long hair and camel's hair coat (Matt. 3:4).

I think Gamaliel, the Pharisee, best captured what a parent's attitude should be about nonspiritually destructive fads: "And so in the present case, I say to you, stay away from these men and let them alone, for if this plan or action is of men, it will be overthrown; but if it is of God, you will not be able to overthrow them; or else you may even be found fighting against God" (Acts 5:38-39).

It is better to allow your teenager to join the Christian "in" crowd or a nondestructive fad than to stomp your foot in ridicule. If it is only a fad, "this too shall pass away." If it is of God — look out!

What About Earrings in a Guy's Ear?

I mentioned the fad of earrings for a guy or a nose ring for a girl. Some of the finest Christian male musicians of today wear an earring in one ear. But most of the musical artists don't. I find the earring distracting, and with our society's difficulties over the battle of the sexes, I wish guys wouldn't wear them. It may limit their acceptance and Christian witness because most older adults don't know how to interpret their wearing an earring. But that is "the gospel according to Ray."

Jesus warned us not to "strain at a gnat and swallow a camel" (Matt. 23:24). Your tirade or command to "get that stupid earring out of your ear right now" may be the reaction to a "gnat." Your teenager's bitterness and anger may be the much larger "camel" that turns him away from the Lord forever.

Be sure you have strong scriptural authority for the things you demand from your kids. Present these demands in a loving way so you don't destroy their love for Jesus and for you. (So David ate the pancakes with catsup until *he* decided they tasted better with syrup!)

What About Rock Music?

When your teenager asks, "What's wrong with listening to rock music?" you should be prepared to give a thorough answer.

Don't be like the woman who placed this ad in the newspaper:

> For sale, cheap. My son's collection of rock 'n' roll records. If a boy's voice answers the phone, please hang up and call later.

Certainly not *all* rock music should be condemned. There are three tests that need to be used for any song or music:

1. Can you clearly understand the lyrics?

Ask yourself, What are the words saying? The words and music often represent the composer's lifestyle. Sexual suggestions and invitations to turn on with drugs abound in many lyrics.

Words not understood at first can, by repetition alone, pass by the *conscious* mind and enter into the listener's *unconscious*, literally brainwashing them.

This is obvious. In fact, *Webster's Encyclopedic Unabridged Dictionary* defines subliminal as "existing or operating below the threshold of consciousness; being or employing stimuli insufficiently intense to produce a discrete sensation but often being or designed to be intense enough to influence the mental processes or the behavior of the individual."

Have you ever caught yourself singing the words of a TV ad jingle or a song that you've heard repeatedly on your car radio? Thinking takes place before singing.

Remember: The Bible is such a "dangerous" book for kids' minds that our courts removed it from public schools many years ago. Yet since that time rock musicians have been allowed in the schools to preach, through their music, the message of a depraved lifestyle which encourages drugs, rebellion, suicide and sexual perversion. Often such messages are piped throughout the lunch hour across the entire school campus. The Bible is *dangerous*, but these songs *aren't?*

A neighbor boy seemed happy and contented as a child. But as he moved into his teen years I would hear discordant rock music blaring from his tape recorder as I shaved each morning. The vocalists told him about an unhappy world of stupid, cruel parents and teachers. They sang in ecstasy about drugs, the occult, rebellion and premarital sex. He quit school in junior high and was placed in a juvenile home for incorrigibles and, later, in a drug rehab center. He grew more and more angry until he finally ran away. Rock music wasn't his only problem, but it was a major contributing factor.

2. How do the combined music and words affect your personality?

Millions of teenagers idolize rock musicians, yet their lifestyles are as depraved as their music. The beat, the tempo and the words possess their very souls. They can do the same to your teenager. They enter the listener's mind and negatively affect his or her mood. As a Christian, I don't want to be negative. Neither should you or your kids.

3. Why would you choose secular music over Christian music?

Have your teenagers been exposed to great Christian music? If they haven't, phone your local contemporary Christian radio station and get the names of the top contemporary Christian artists. Go out and buy two or three of their cassettes. Give them to your kids without a lecture. Just say, "I love you. I thought you might enjoy these." Then pray and let God take over from there.

Yes, it will be the same loud volume and thumping beat. You still won't understand some of the lyrics. But it's the *right message.*

How to Get This Across to Your Kids

Sit down with your teenagers and calmly discuss the three tests just listed. Then have them turn the radio on to their favorite rock station and carefully explain to you the lyrics of *the next ten songs played*. Do the same thing with MTV or any rock music. Often you'll find them blushing about what the disc jockey is saying, not to mention the lyrics. You'll have made your point.

Two names to remember if you want your kids to choose the right types of music: 1) Jesus Christ. Pray for your kids to make the right decisions about music on their own with Christ's help; and 2) Al Menconi. Al's "Media Update" is the finest newsletter on music that I have ever seen. Just call (619) 591-4696 and ask for a free sample. Also, Al's book *Today's Music: A Window to Your Child's Soul* is great reading for any parent.

What About the Movies?

Watching a movie or television program with your kids and discussing it afterward over Cokes can be a very healthy bonding experience as long as four things are remembered:

1. If you sat through a movie with explicit sexual scenes or excessive violence without walking out, your kids will interpret your actions as approval of the movie.

2. If they know you go to movies you do not allow them to see, your kids may think you are a hypocrite.

3. Movie ratings are very subjective. They certainly aren't evaluated with biblical standards in mind. Remember that responses to situations displayed on the screen will affect the way your teenager responds to his or her own real-life situations. This is particularly true for teens who are just beginning to date and are looking for standards of appropriate dating behavior.

4. Filthy language is contagious, especially if "heroes" talk that way. It is Christian wisdom to avoid filthy language (Eph. 5:4).

Family Entertainment?

Lead your family to make "a covenant with their eyes" as Job did:

> I have made a covenant with my eyes. How then could I gaze at a [woman or girl] (Job 31:1, brackets added)?

Here are a couple of resources that can save you time and money and provide the best in film entertainment. Feature Films for Families produces and sells feature-length movies that are very unique and low-priced. Their films do not contain any profanity, vulgarity, graphic violence or nudity. All of their films reinforce positive Christian values. This company believes the human mind is greatly affected by what the five senses receive. They have an ever-increasing quantity of video movies for distribution. They can be reached at 1-800-347-2833.

A video store can offer a million choices. To narrow the choice, ask if they have films which are recommended by the Dove Foundation. The Dove Foundation is a nonprofit, family-advocacy organization that recommends "family-friendly entertainment." You can get their latest catalog *free* (containing a list of their recommended videos plus all the video stores that carry them) by calling (616) 554-9993.

> Finally, brethren, whatever is true, whatever is honorable, whatever is right, whatever is pure, whatever is lovely, whatever is of good repute, if there is any excellence and if anything worthy of praise, let your mind dwell on these things (Phil. 4:8).

Let *that* be your movie and TV guide!

Not all the dummies in the movies get thrown over the cliffs!

Dear Ray:

I'm a stepdad who wishes my stepson were my own son. Charlie, at nine, is mentally messed up from a dad who verbally tore him apart constantly. He seems to hate himself. His mom and I love him a lot, but we aren't sure what to do.

Please tell us how we can help him build a sense of his own worth in Christ. I don't think he'll make it to adulthood otherwise.

We've read *Marriage Plus*, and we even got a whole lot out of *Singles Plus*. We're thrilled you're doing a book on raising kids now. I'll read it over and over again. Thanks.

Wanting a New Beginning
for My Stepson

Death and life are in
the power of the tongue.
Proverbs 18:21

NINE

YOUR WORD
IS YOUR BOND

No wonder kids are all mixed up.
Half the time they are being told to
"find themselves," and the other half
they're being told to "get lost"!

I HAD TO laugh at the sign in my veterinarian's waiting room. It read: "Doctor will be with you shortly. Sit! Stay!" I read it and did.

It's vital that you recognize how important words are between a parent and a child. The dictionary says *talk* means "to utter words." To *communicate* means "to transfer thoughts." This book you're holding will do you no good unless it *communicates*. But neither will a parent's words unless they do the same.

As we communicate on the subject of bonding we must remember: A major part of self-control is mouth control (James 1:19-20).

165

Rave Reviews

A "rave review" is a great review. So let's review what our great God has given us as absolute essentials for bonding with our kids.

1. Don't fight.

2. Treat your kids equally.

3. Never lie to your kids.

4. Be parents who are obviously in love with each other.

5. Work to keep an atmosphere of fun and fellowship between you and your kids.

6. Treat all your children's friends as welcome visitors in the house.

7. Always answer your kids' questions.

We'll complete the ten rules for bonding in this chapter.

Managers Needed

When speaking of the Christian leader who is also a father, Paul says: "He must be one who manages his own household well, keeping his children under control with all dignity" (1 Tim. 3:4).

Paul defines Christian church leadership as "a fine work" (1 Tim. 3:1), and in establishing the qualifications of deacons he writes, "Let deacons be husbands of only one wife, and good managers of their children and their own households" (1 Tim. 3:12).

God insists that dads be good managers of their own homes: "But if a man does not know how to manage his own household, how will he take care of the church of God?" (1 Tim. 3:5).

God says a dad can't minister effectively to a church if he isn't ministering effectively at home. It's sheer hypocrisy to live like a lost person away from the church and pretend to be a Christian in the church. Hypocrisy turns people away from Christ.

Two things create the picture of "Christian" hypocrisy:

1. Sinful actions: A hypocrite is a person who *prays* on Sunday but *preys* on others the rest of the week.

2. Spoken words: People who aren't *smart* say things that do.

David prayed a prayer all Christian parents should pray: "Set a guard, O Lord, over my mouth; keep watch over the door of my lips" (Ps. 141:3). Another way to pray that is, "Lord, don't let my mouth go into motion until my spirit is in gear!"

8. Needed for bonding: Never correct or punish your kids in the presence of other people.

It's essential to make positive communication a part of your dinner hour with your kids. A great communication-starter is: "What was the happiest thing that happened to you today?" Let everybody take a turn answering — including Mom and Dad.

Mothers are going to ask, "What about correcting manners at the table?" That's not where to do it. We have millions of ruined digestive tracts throughout America because of this mistake!

Instead, call a 4 P.M. weeklong drill. Tell your children you've noticed some table manners that will become a real embarrassment to them if they don't stop. Then, Monday through Friday of the next week, meet with your child at the table each day at 4 P.M. to work on correcting the problem manners. Tell them that if they overcome the problem, this will be the only week needed for the 4 P.M. drill. They'll work like crazy to get their manners right, because they're not going to want a second week of drill.

Since children learn good table manners by observing good table manners, keep yours sharpened too. Make sure the whole family eats a meal together almost every night. Keep your television turned off when you are having dinner. (If that turns dad off, change the time for dinner!) Save that time for positive family communication.

Correct and Incorrect Corrections

In *The Family Book of Manners*, Hermine Hartley says, "Manners are more than using the right fork. They're using the right attitude.

167

Our behavior can affect our relationships much more than our etiquette."[1]

Kids hear *what* you are saying, but they also read *how* you are saying it — your tone of voice, the look on your face and your body language.

Never correct your children or teenagers in the presence of others, including other children or teenagers, if it can be avoided. This can bring instant embarrassment and bitterness that may last a lifetime.

One question I'm routinely asked is, "How do I keep from punishing my child in front of others while in a department store or a supermarket?"

Foster Cline and Jim Fay answered that question in *Parenting With Love and Logic*. They explain how kids, even before they can speak, learn the situations in which their parents are vulnerable. That's why the little darlings become so adept at picking the store, the restaurant or the Sunday church service to disobey or throw a tantrum. They learn that Mom or Dad will not resort to embarrassing correction in public, so they enjoy a field day while they can.

Cline and Fay present a technique called the "Strategic Training Session" for dealing with this situation:

> Laura tried it with her daughter Holly. She phoned her best friend one evening and said, "I've been having trouble with Holly when I go shopping, and I need your help. Would you station yourself at the pay phone outside the store tomorrow morning at 10:30? I have a feeling you're going to get a call." Laura then filled her friend in on the plan.
>
> The next day Laura and Holly went shopping, and true to form, Holly became her usual obnoxious self even before the automatic doors of the store had closed behind them.
>
> In a quiet voice, Laura said, "Holly, would you rather behave or go sit in your room?"
>
> Holly looked quizzically at her mom as if to say, "Get real, Mom. You'd take me home after you've come all the way down here to shop?" Then she ratcheted her attack up a notch.

The next thing Holly knew she was being led to a pay phone in the store where Laura dialed a number and said, "Shopping is not fun today. Please come."

Thirty seconds later, Holly's eyes grew big as pie plates when her mom's friend strolled through the door, took Holly's hand, and said, "Let's go to your room. You can wait for your mom there."

Holly was escorted home and sent to her room. Laura was freed to make her rounds in unhurried bliss. Holly was allowed out of her room when Laura returned. She was very happy to see her mom again, while Laura taught her little girl that, even in public, obnoxious behavior has consequences.[2]

The authors make the point as clearly as it can be made: "There is absolutely no reason for kids to get away with hellish behavior simply because we're with them."

What If I'm Alone?

You might be saying, But I don't have a friend close enough to give me that kind of help. OK. Face Ferdinand or Snoodvilla by yourself. Face this, too: Either you or your children are going to be in charge. God and I vote for you. That's why you are the parent and they are the children (see Eph. 6:1-4). What they are doing is a real crime.

Again, take them anywhere unimportant to you but make a big deal out of how great this outing can be. But warn them that at the first sign of rebellion, by words or actions, they will be going home fast. Keep your word. Every time they act up in the slightest, take them home and send them to their room. They will tire of this very fast and discover neither crime nor rebellion pays. Soon you'll have a happy traveling companion who will brighten your days as a parent.

Aren't These Methods Cruel?

These methods aren't cruel. "Cruel" is teaching kids there are *no consequences* for their sins or misbehavior. "Cruel" is the treatment such a spoiled child will eventually give his or her parents and all

169

others who are in a position of authority, including God. "Cruel" is also when a parent loses patience and slaps the child silly. "Cruel" is the treatment that child will suffer in this world — and perhaps the next — because his parents didn't love him enough to discipline him. "Cruel" things happen when a kid goes out of control and doesn't receive godly discipline.

God wants you to "train" your children — not humiliate them. Verbal abuse is child abuse. Many parents who won't spank their children do far more emotional damage with their tongue.

Much more will be written about spankings in chapter 12, but remember: *Never* spank or verbally correct your child in front of others. If you do, any kid who is observing is likely to tell your kid later, "You sure have a mean parent!" You don't want that kind of bad advertising.

When talking with anyone (including me) about your kids' behavior or about appropriate discipline, ask your questions *in private, without your children listening.* Otherwise they will be humiliated — or take notes and test you on it!

9. Needed for bonding: Concentrate on your child's good points. Don't overemphasize his or her failings.

You like to be liked. So do your kids. Too often parents blow up at the F's and ignore the A+'s. Instead, consider the dad who examined his son's terrible report card and remarked, "Well, one thing is definitely in your favor. With this report card you couldn't possibly be cheating!"

> The good man out of his good treasure brings forth what is good; and the evil man out of his evil treasure brings forth what is evil. And I say to you, that every careless word that men shall speak, they shall render account for it in the day of judgment. For by your words you shall be justified, and by your words you shall be condemned (Matt. 12:35-37).

The Greek word for *careless* in the term *careless word* means "unproductive word." A careless word is not in agreement with God's Word. It does not do what God intended words to do. God created words for healing and wholeness. When, instead, they are used in a way that harms or kills (Prov. 18:21a), the one speaking is bringing condemnation upon himself unless he repents.

Thank God once again for the only "cleanser" strong enough to delete any careless words we've spoken — the blood of Christ. Ask the Lord — and anyone you've offended (including members of your own family) — to forgive you for any careless words. Then quit saying them. At that point the Lord will "cleanse you from all unrighteousness" (1 John 1:9).

Your Words Have Mighty Power

> Truly I say to you, whoever says to this mountain, "Be taken up and cast into the sea," and does not doubt in his heart, but believes that what he says is going to happen; it shall be granted him (Mark 11:23).
>
> Now in the morning, when He returned to the city, He became hungry. And seeing a lone fig tree by the road, He came to it and found nothing on it except leaves only; and He said to it, "No longer shall there ever be any fruit from you." And at once the fig tree withered (Matt. 21:18-19).

Christ's words are powerful. And with His power, your words can add health — spiritual, mental and physical — to your kids' lives or wither them. It's up to you (Prov. 18:21).

There are certain words that deeply injure the human spirit. Never tag your family members or anyone else with negative words or titles. For example, here are some words to eliminate from your vocabulary. Never use these words (or words like them) on your kids again.

Stupid or *dumb*. A friend and I were having a wonderful visit together. Then we got on one subject where he was trying to explain something to me. Suddenly, in frustration, he stopped and said, "I'm just dumb!" He wasn't dumb at all. He had simply believed a negative label someone had placed on him when he was a kid, and he had been wearing it ever since. We tend to act out what we really believe about ourselves.

Clumsy. Don't call your child or teenager clumsy. I guarantee you that every teenager is going to knock over the milk — it will happen! Teenagers are growing every minute. They have body parts they can't even identify. Their arms seem to grow longer by the week. The milk is going to go down. Just be prepared for it. When your teenager knocks it over, just have a good laugh and help them clean it up.

Lazy. Children or teenagers aren't "lazy" because they sleep until ten o'clock on Saturday mornings. Most kids never get enough sleep during the week. So they try a "crash course" on Saturdays! Just be sure you have some chores lined up for them to do when they do wake up. But don't call them lazy.

"You're bad," or *"You little devil."* Never say "You're a *bad* boy!" or "You're a *bad* girl!" or "You little *devil!*" The devil isn't little, and he loves to hear his name used like that. Don't put those types of thoughts into anyone's head — especially a child's. Harsh words only drive the problems deeper. Teach them. Change their bad behavior. Be their example. But don't call them bad.

"He's just *shy*. One negative phrase parents often use when a young child doesn't warm up to a stranger is "He's just shy." Don't say that. The truth is that a child who doesn't warm up to strangers is very typical and probably safer. If you don't call attention to his momentary stage of withdrawal, you will most likely see him pull out of it a little later in life and be perfectly at ease with others.

Shut up. "Shut up" is the closest many Christians come to swearing. It is nearly always spoken with the same intensity as a harsh swear word. When you say it to anyone — most of all, to a kid — you may have silenced him, but not effectively. You have verbally slapped and humiliated him. Ask forgiveness for these words immediately. If you don't, your child may get bitter and retaliate in the same way toward you or others.

Listen to Yourself for a Full Day

Be sure your praise heavily outweighs any negative comments. Build a healthy self-image into each kid. No one ever "nagged" a person into receiving Jesus! I recommend that every parent read Zig Ziglar's book *Raising Positive Kids in a Negative World*. Zig and I agree — kids are born to win!

Applause! Applause!

Hang up the pictures and school work your child does so that the whole world can see and applaud. Of course, to tell the truth, Arlyne and I were a bit worried about David at the age of four. We didn't know what the pictures he was drawing meant. But then one day we came across the works of Pablo Picasso, and we were suddenly convinced we were raising a genius!

Matter-of-factly praise your kids' positive Christian actions and attitudes. Soon you'll see them doing this to others (Luke 6:31), and this happy attitude will become a wonderful part of their general outlook on life.

10. Needed for bonding: Be consistent in your affection and your moods.

> But the fruit of the Spirit is love, joy, peace, patience, kindness, goodness, faithfulness, gentleness, self-control; against such things there is no law (Gal. 5:22-23).

My cousins Mike and Marian Bever own an apple orchard in Washington. They tell me they have never heard even one apple tree grunt and groan while it was producing an apple! Fruit from healthy trees just grows naturally and without strain. That's how "the fruit of the Spirit" is meant to grow too. Exhibit this fruit consistently and equally with your kids so they can see Christ in you. It will assure them strong mental health in adulthood and cause them to want a relationship with Jesus Christ like yours.

Imperfect Teenagers

Here are two effective ways to keep an older teenager home: Make the environment pleasant — and let the air out of his or her tires!

As a parent, you may feel you have lost touch with how your teen really thinks these days. It is easy to get back in touch — take a look at his or her room. Hieroglyphics never told archaeologists as much about ancient civilizations as the walls of your teenager's bedroom can tell you about him (or her). You'll discover who his heroes are and where his interest is really focused.

A Desire for "Perfection"

Like all of us, teenagers make mistakes. But few adults demand "perfection" in themselves as a teenager does. They do not need a parent constantly reminding them of their mistakes. Negative words reinforce negative feelings and actions, and make your teens certain they'll "never get it right."

Majoring on the minors — picking on the little mistakes as if they were mountains — causes many teenagers to quit trying to live the Christian life. Obvious sin must be confronted. But if a child misses making his bed one day or spills the milk, your loving response will go a long way toward causing that child to be glad you are his parent.

Signs of the Times

When our kids left their beds unmade or their rooms messy, Arlyne would hang handwritten, multicolored signs on their bedroom doors. Among my all-time favorites was: "If things aren't put away — big blue wrecking crew will attack this bedroom at 7 P.M. this evening. Beware!"

Arlyne considered their schedules and gave them a realistic amount of time to get the room cleaned up or the bed made. Larry tells of a time when he'd left a mess and ignored the warning. Arriving home later, he discovered the whole mess piled on top of his bed. It was only after he had put everything away that he was able to go to bed — very late! Larry learned his lesson and knew Arlyne meant what she said, even if it was written on a funny sign!

Give Them Space

Teenagers like to be alone at times. They need to sort out thoughts, get new ideas and become "their own person." It is part of the weaning process that will continue throughout the teen years. But it may feel like rejection to the parents.

During this time kids often prefer being with their friends over being with their parents. Their formative years will bear fruit as they learn to make their own godly choices as teenagers. The Christian teenager who loves the Lord, the Bible, his Christian friends and church gives little sorrow and great joy to Christian parents.

If at all possible, your teenager needs his or her own bedroom, or at least his own space within the bedroom. Yet even as I write this I remember years when our boys were all together in one room and the girls in another. It didn't hurt them. It taught them to share. I remember Tim's saying once, "When I get married, I'll only marry a woman who will sleep on the floor with me!" His wife changed that idea.

If kids do share a room, it is vital to teach them to honor each other's property and space — and not to borrow anything without first getting permission from the owner.

A teenager's bedroom becomes his or her sanctuary. The teen needs to keep it orderly, and it is never a place for sin. But it should be *his* or *her* room.

Exaggerated Feelings and Emotions

Teenagers are often led by their heroes. This can be good or bad, depending on whom they choose to follow. Worldly heroes and idols manipulate the young to buy into their sinful lifestyles by appealing to the fantasy of a whole new world beyond the restraints of parental control. But once a teenager finds himself bound to a devastating life experience or addiction, the hideous reality explodes around him. By then, without Christ, it is often too late to do anything except suffer the full and terrible consequences of his lost choices.

Teenagers' emotions are intense. They tend to be very idealistic, and when their dreams are shattered they often see life as hopeless. That's one reason why suicide is a leading killer of young people between the ages of fifteen and twenty-four. In their young minds they believe negative experiences can't change and life can't get better.

If Jesus Christ is not their strength, they have no strength. Thus the devil finds great delight in tormenting the mind of an unhappy teenager.

When a teenager does find himself trapped in the valley of despair and his world seems to be falling apart, he needs to recognize what we all need to remember:

God is our refuge and strength, a very present help in trouble (Ps. 46:1).

Jesus Christ and parents who have really bonded with their kids make the winning team against all odds.

Raising kids is like drafting a blueprint — you have to know where to draw the lines.

Dear Ray:

I have three teenagers. The eldest is a natural-born mechanic. My middle child is the preacher in our family. And our youngest likes to sit a lot and think (mostly sit). I don't have a lot of money, and the two older teens are one and two years away from college. Shall I rob a bank? Should my wife and I borrow and put ourselves in debt for the rest of our lives?

Should each student take a college loan when it's his turn? How important is college for each of them anyway? Is it worth our going broke?

Parents With More
Questions Than Money

Be diligent to present yourself
approved to God as a workman
who does not need to be
ashamed, handling accurately
the word of truth.
2 Timothy 2:15

TEN

How Essential Is School?

The college campus of today
is one of the greatest
supporters of wildlife!

HOW ESSENTIAL IS school?" It sounds like a strange question, but I'm asked it all the time by kids. Some of them are hoping I'll say it isn't essential at all. Others are hoping I can talk their parents into sending them to Harvard! The answer lies somewhere in between.

This is not our nation's finest hour. Nor is it like "the good old days." You might not be reading this book if Mrs. Holly Geary had not kept me after school every day in the fourth grade to write stories that she had me read aloud the next day to the entire class. I wasn't being punished. She just wanted to meet an honest need in me — and she did!

Ken Wallace, my high school drama coach, had "heart to hearts" with me that bonded him to me as my favorite teacher of all time. His high moral values, ethical standards and great encouragement helped me through the hassles and heartaches so common during the school "daze."

Today, though there are still marvelous exceptions, it's not like that in most public schools. Too often teachers are living lifestyles that any Christian would consider unacceptable. Many are not concerned about the real needs of the kids. They are far more interested in themselves and their own liberal philosophies. From individual teachers with personal problems to a consolidated mass voice which demands radical change, they attempt to reshape the destiny of kids today. Since most of them have tenure, their jobs remain unthreatened.

The National Education Association is riddled with hedonists and humanists sold out to the type of social changes Christians can't accept. It makes one realize that not all educated people are intelligent!

Most public schools today add to the division of state and home. Condoms and "free" abortions upon request replace moral values and lead kids into immorality. Situational ethics ("Do whatever works, whether it's ethical or not") replaces concrete ethical standards. Even if teachers support traditional values, they often work in overcrowded schools filled with rebellious, angry, volatile students who abuse their teachers with everything from words to guns. Ironically, using the Lord's name as a swear word is OK in many schools, but talking about Him *isn't!*

School Dazed

For the wrath of God is revealed from heaven against all ungodliness and unrighteousness of men, who suppress the truth in unrighteousness, *because that which is known about God is evident within them*; for God made it evident to them. For since the creation of the world His invisible attributes, His eternal power and divine nature, have been clearly seen, being understood through what has been made, so that they are without excuse. For even though they knew God, they did not honor Him as

God, or give thanks; but they became futile in their speculations, and their foolish heart was darkened. Professing to be wise, they became fools (Rom.1:18-22, italics added).

Professing to be wise in the worldly sense, our public schools have moved closer to foolishness. *U.S News & World Report* magazine put it this way:

> The typical high school student's schedule — 1st period: Driver's ed; 2nd period: AIDS awareness; 3rd period: Counseling — is looking less and less like a classical education. On average, the National Education Commission on Time and Learning reported high schools require students to spend barely 41 percent of classroom time on academic subjects. The commission counts three hours a day for English, science, math, civics, languages, or history...To boost basic class time to five and a half hours, the panel suggested curbing summer vacation...All of this, Education Secretary Richard Riley noted, involves changing the "structure and rhythm of American life."[1]

It is precisely the changing of "the structure of American life" that needs to be examined by Christian parents. Our kids' eternal souls are at stake. Obviously, learning is extremely important. But *what* you learn is equally important.

Outcome-Based Education (OBE)

One of the newest educational fads, outcome-based education (OBE), was designed by William G. Spady, a sociologist who has never taught school. Twenty years ago, the similar philosophy of mastery learning was introduced, but it failed to have a significant impact. Both of these approaches attempt to bring attitudinal changes. OBE strongly enforces the antibiblical, "no absolutes" philosophy discussed earlier in this book.

Psychiatrist Jeffrey Burke Satinover, former fellow at the Child Study Center at Yale University and a private-practice psychotherapist, sees several problems with OBE:

> Upwards of 50 percent of the "outcomes" being "meas-
> ured" by OBE are attitudinal. Forget whether you agree
> or disagree with the attitudes being promoted...As an
> educational objective for children, such an "outcome"
> will encourage acquiescence to whatever passes as the
> politically correct stop-thought of the moment.
>
> Since these outcomes are found in nationally distrib-
> uted OBE curricula, the result will be children who all
> have been trained to think the same way about major
> social questions. That is, in the way that OBE proponents
> want them to think....
>
> OBE will strip local school boards — and hence par-
> ents — of their already significantly eroded authority and
> control, and transfer this authority directly to State, and,
> indirectly, Federal bureaucrats.
>
> States are encouraged [by OBE] to pass legislation
> that, with few minor exceptions, *eliminates all cur-
> rent statutes pertaining to education*...The result:
> a greater degree of uniformity in attitudes among
> individuals, and a lower level of overall excellence in
> academics.[2]

Conservative activist Phyllis Schlafly says OBE will treat "students as guinea pigs" in a radical experiment: "It offers no method
of accountability to students, parents, teachers or taxpayers. Educators admit OBE is very expensive. In the elementary grades OBE
does not teach children essential reading, writing and arithmetic
skills."[3]

All of this is particularly interesting in the light of the continually lowering test scores and achievement results that yearly embarrass most of America's public schools. Small wonder many
educators want to get away from the subjects they don't know how
to teach!

Meanwhile, almost all Christian schools have kept their academic standards high by using the kinds of curricula popular in the
1950s, a time when the Bible, prayer and good study habits were
"in," and no one needed a metal detector to stay safe.

Choosing Your Kids' Schools

Teaching children *how* to count isn't nearly as important as teaching children *what* counts. Right from the start, an educational system isn't worth a great deal if it teaches kids how to make a living, but it doesn't teach them how to live.

Parents today must carefully consider all options before they hand their child over to a school or teacher who believes a child's basic reading, writing or math skills are far less important than whether the child accepts radical feminism and homosexuality as valuable lifestyles. Beyond this, Christian parents must decide exactly how important all Christian values really are.

To avoid the humanistic indoctrination of your child or teenager, consider sending them to a Christian elementary or high school. Academically, private schools are usually far superior to public schools. Spiritually, Christ-centered teachers, who know that their ministry is helping each kid grow in the Lord, are some of the finest gifts God has sent to this earth.

In spite of the financial sacrifice it took, Arlyne and I will forever praise the Lord that Tim, Elizabeth and David spent nearly all of their elementary years in Christian schools. They were able to go to secular high schools because each had had such outstanding Christian training during the formative years. The Mossholder kids were popular with students and teachers, and though they weren't "preachy," they were known for following, believing and sharing the Lord.

One word of caution: Be sure the Christian school where you send your kids really *is* Christian. Teachers in a Christian school should be well-educated; good communicators; deeply caring about both their students and their students' parents; know, believe and teach God's Word; and know how God's Word pertains to whatever else they teach. A school full of such teachers is worth its weight in gold.

Home schooling is another excellent alternative to public schools. Not only does it offer great opportunities for daily bonding in parent-child or teen relationships, but it is usually far less expensive than formal Christian schools. An excellent resource list for those interested in home schooling is available through Focus on the Family.

Another word of caution: Know yourself, parent! One precious mother told me, "I could never home school. I'm not organized enough or educated enough. Besides, if it were a beautiful day outside, I'm the kind of person who would simply shout, 'School's out!'" Your kids deserve a real education whichever kind of school they attend.

How Well Does Your Family Know Christ?

Now you are Christ's body, and individually members of it (1 Cor. 12:27).

Families in a church are very individual. Some families have certain members who aren't interested in Christ. Some families are brand-new Christians. Still other families have known Christ for a long time and, from the oldest to the youngest, serve Him with great joy. This fact may have a great deal to do with how a family decides which type of school to attend. The new Christians may need strong protection from the radical philosophies found today in many public schools from kindergarten on. But a Christ-centered family may see this as a great opportunity to bring God's truths into a world of horrendous philosophical darkness.

Christians are to be *salt* (Matt. 5:13); the *light* of the world; and a city on a hill that *can't be hidden* (Matt. 5:14). In Matthew 5:16 Christ said, "Let your light shine before men in such a way that they may see your good works, and glorify your Father who is in heaven."

The goal of the Christian is to be a shining light so that others who see that light will meet Christ and learn to glorify God too.

Far more than talent motivates a Carman or a Jack Hayford or a Ben Kinchlow. It is the same thing which causes a Ruth Elliott, Gloria Gaither or Terry Meeuwsen to shine. They are people who will *not* let their lights stay hidden (Matt. 5:15). Many children and teenagers are just like them.

Christ in you, the hope of glory (Col. 1:27).

Do you look at your Christian kids and think: There's the hope of glory? You should. Do you look at yourself in the mirror and think: There's the hope of glory?! You should.

One mark of a mature Christian is that his or her light is not hidden. Use your unique gifts and talents to shine for God and teach your kids to do the same thing.

Obviously, Christians are never to be conceited or puffed-up braggarts. A big-mouthed, bragging churchgoer is like a rooster crowing in the middle of the night — you'd prefer them fried!

Teachers, school administrators and all in public education need Jesus Christ. Perhaps your kids are ready to share Christ with them, if not by words, then by their lifestyle. Be realistic about this. Don't force your kids to witness verbally. But as Hannah gave her son, Samuel, to the Lord (1 Sam. 1:28) and then to Eli, whose "school" was far less than desirable (1 Sam. 1:25-28; 2:12), Samuel grew to be a mighty man of God.

As Christ's salt (Matt. 5:13), if your kids are attending a public school, get involved with the PTA. If possible, get elected to the school board. Even if you are not on the school board, attend and participate in the meetings. Show Christ's love and share biblical principles with them.

Why Is This So Important?

Witnessing means to share Jesus Christ with others. Yet 95 percent of Christians have never led even one person to Christ.[4] Christians stay mute because 1) they don't know exactly what to say; or 2) they are afraid to say it.

> When the Holy Spirit has come upon you...you shall be My witnesses (Acts 1:8).

Christ has called you to be His witness.

Your Family Should Be a Power Pack

We'll get right back to the subject of schools, but far too few families have ever learned how to share their faith in Christ.

For a moment let's concentrate on how the Holy Spirit can make your family ready to share Christ at school or anywhere.

Many years ago, when I was a church youth director, I assembled from the teenagers in our group what we called "a power pack." These teenagers would accompany me to churches and share three things with the congregations:

1. What their lives were like before they received Christ.

2. How they met Christ.

3. What happened in their lives as a result of meeting Christ.

Those kids were a powerful witness. Adults and kids gave their lives to Christ by the dozens because of these witnesses and their testimonies.

That's what your family is meant to do. No matter which school they attend, your kids should be a power pack.

Eighty-six percent of church growth is because of friendship/relational evangelism.[5] The greatest evangelistic tool in America is also its most wasted resource — the American family.

You Don't Have to "Make a Sale"

Christ is not demanding that you close a sale when you share Him with others. Witnessing is not "the gathering of scalps"! The average person who comes to Christ had eight encounters with the gospel before making a decision for Him.[6] Once in a while you will have the incredible joy of being the one who leads someone to Christ. More often you'll simply be one who plants a seed. Only 5 percent of Christians have ever won a person to Christ. You'd better get started! So should your kids.

Ask These Family Questions

Call a special family night when everyone is home and can take part. Sing Christian songs together, pray together and ask each person to share the answers to the power-pack questions. Be sure every Christian in your home — no matter how young — shares his or her own experience.

When you have all shared, be sure everyone understands you have just "witnessed" to each other.

Now have each person organize these answers into a seven-minute testimony, or less for very young children. Parents will need to help their younger children write down their answers.

Many people mistakenly think only dramatic testimonies (ax murderers and drug addicts) will interest anyone else. If the Lord has redeemed you from pits like these, share the truth. But often the greatest testimonies are from those who came to Christ as children or remained faithful with only minor temptations and problems. God's faithfulness and preservation are a great testimony.

Question 1 of your testimony is actually the least important part. Share it because it will tell others what you were saved out of. But far more important is how Christ has challenged and changed your life since you were saved. Lost people can't share anything like that.

Help each family member decide on someone outside your family with whom to share his or her testimony one-on-one. Each of you should choose a different person. It's all right if this first person is already a Christian.

If you do share with a Christian, teach the person how to make a seven-minute outline of his own. Continue sharing with more people.

By the time you have shared your seven-minute testimony with two or three others, begin to pray about an unsaved person with whom to share it next.

Be prayed up, then go ahead. After you have shared, ask the person if he or she would like to receive Christ too.

Remember: You don't have to make a sale. You've planted a seed. Now keep planting that seed in others.

Do Kids Need College or University?

Any of us would like to be able to buy a Mercedes out of our petty cash. But consider this: According to the Economic Policy Institute, a Washington research organization which issues a book-length report on "The State of Working America" every two years, there was a huge college-high school wage gap during most of the 1980s.

Many of the high-school-educated were blue-collar workers in manufacturing where employment declined....But in 1989 the nation entered another period of weak economic growth and recession, one that lasted until the spring of 1991. This time, however, the wages of the college-educated did not bounce back when the recession ended.

The wages of men with bachelor's degrees have continued to deteriorate at least into 1993 despite an increasingly robust economy that began in the spring of 1991....Only college-educated women have gained ground on inflation, but their wages are still lower than those of men with BAs, whose median hourly wage in 1993 had slipped to $17.62. Adjusted for inflation, the decline was about 3 percent since 1989. "I don't see any reason this trend should have changed since 1993 or will change in the near future," said Lawrence Mishel, research director of the Economic Policy Institute.

"Another message from the study is that putting people to work...(despite the creation of more than 4 million jobs since President Clinton took office)...no longer translates easily into higher living standards. Indeed, college graduates have taken jobs in rising numbers, and, as a result, the total wages paid to all college graduates have risen," Mishel said. "But because the money has to be spread over so many people, the typical college graduate finds that his income has not kept up with inflation," he said. And this remains the case even when the amounts that employers pay for pensions and health insurance are added in.

Wages, Mishel said, are held back by "structural" factors — including weak unions, a proliferation of low-wage industries, competition from foreign labor, too little improvement in productivity or efficiency, and a minimum wage that is too low. This in turn pulls down the entire pay scale, he said.[7]

In spite of the above, it may yet be true, if money could buy happiness, every person should earn an advanced degree.

But some people who never got past a high school education earn more in a lifetime than most university graduates. The amount of education a person gets is not as much of an indicator of success as one might think. It is estimated that over 80 percent of university graduates in America are earning their living ten years later in fields completely unrelated to their majors in school!

Thomas Alva Edison suffered from a lack of hearing during childhood. "At age six, he came home from school one day with a note from his teacher suggesting he be taken out of school because he was 'too stupid to learn.' "[8] Later, about the lighting of the very first street lights, Mr. Edison reportedly said: "If I had had a formal education, I would have known that it is impossible to make a lightbulb!"

Christ's students can attend any school as salt. But God warns all Christians in Colossians 2:8: "See to it that no one takes you captive through philosophy and empty deception, according to the tradition of men, according to the elementary principles of the world, rather than according to Christ."

Secular colleges and universities are rampant with humanism, evolution, atheism and other vain philosophies, plus coed dorms. Condom vending machines are available in both restrooms and laundry rooms at most of these schools.[9]

Recently a father lamented to me, "My two kids went to church until they left our home for college. Their mom and I saw them change almost immediately. Today they refuse to go to church, they laugh at our Christianity, and they have become snobbish, educated atheists." This happens far too often. "The lust of the flesh and the lust of the eyes and the boastful pride of life" have deceived them (1 John 2:15-17).

Thank God for Campus Crusade for Christ, Chi Alpha, New Generation Campus Ministries, Baptist Student Union and other outstanding Christian organizations found on many college and university campuses. They often provide an oasis in a desert of philosophy and empty deception. Any student would be wise to seek out these organizations.

Uneducated?

It is God who has ordained each day of our lives (Ps. 139:16). As we seek Him He will guide us to choose His plan for success (Jer. 29:11). If a person goes through life and only makes money, he is not a success.

College is not an automatic necessity for everyone's life. But if it seems to be part of God's plan for your son or daughter, here are some vital questions to ponder:

1. Would the school they are considering have a positive or negative effect on their commitment to and love for the Lord?

3. Is there a Bible college or university that could give them as good or better training in their chosen field? The financial costs of attending a Christian school will be higher than those of a secular state school, but the spiritual benefits can more than make up for that.

4. If you plan to support them financially through college, have they exhibited the kind of hard work in high school that convinces you they will work diligently in college? If not, but they still want to go to a secular school, perhaps they should attend a community college for the first two years to prove their self-discipline and capability. A community college can also be the answer for those students who want to get their university-required general education courses out of the way at a fraction of the expense a university charges. They can be employed during their first two years of college, save up for their two years or more of university and continue to pray for God's guidance concerning their future.

5. If you do support them financially through college, and they don't know Jesus Christ now, will college make them better-educated sinners, who are "sure" they will never need the Lord (Deut. 8:18-20)?

Things to Remember

Unless students are sure they are going into some form of ministry and will not be seeking a secular career, those who attend college will probably need to attend an accredited college or university. Even some ministry positions require an accredited education.

If your son or daughter isn't led by the Lord to attend a four-year college, it will be important for them to develop a skill. Trade schools, training schools and apprenticeship programs which usually require far less than four years can often provide a well-paying skill even during an economic depression.

Today, because of downsizing and the phasing out of certain jobs, it may be more important to be a "jack of all trades" than to be "the master of one." Predictions are that machinery will keep on replacing manpower. In the future most people will work two or three jobs during a week rather than stay focused in one career.

Bible Colleges and Universities

There are many outstanding Bible colleges and universities throughout America. Tim graduated from L.I.F.E. Bible College in Los Angeles (now located in San Dimas), California. He received a master's degree in ministry from Azusa Pacific University, which is another fine Christian college in Southern California. Elizabeth graduated from Oral Roberts University in Tulsa, Oklahoma, where David plans to graduate next year. All three have been extremely well-trained in their fields. I highly recommend these schools.

Beyond that, my kids have a great knowledge of the Lord and how He relates to what they have learned. They love Him and are very thankful for His strong hand of guidance and blessing on their life's work.

Regent University in Virginia Beach, Virginia, offers outstanding graduate studies. It is superior in several fields to most secular graduate schools in many ways.

Should Students Take College Loans?

The rich rules over the poor,
And the borrower becomes the lender's slave (Prov. 22:7).

At the present time, college loans carry a very low interest rate. But that rate, coupled with the full amount of the loan, may take a very long time to repay.

Before borrowing any money for any reason, prayerfully and

191

carefully consider all the ramifications. What is the full amount to be repaid? What is the time allowed for repayment? What is the possibility and penalty of not being able to make the payments? What is the guaranteed return as a benefit of the money borrowed?

Many college graduates have shared with me the difficulty of repaying their college loans. Marriage, missionary work, graduate studies or other important life choices have been put on an extended hold in order to pay the debt. Still others married and began raising their families only to discover themselves deeply in debt and unable to provide adequately for their families.

The government is still working on creative ways to pay back student loans, including seasons of service for graduates. But it is never wise to "become the lender's slave."

Earning Your Way Through College

The things we pay for ourselves are the things we appreciate most. When parents put their kids through school, the value will often be greatly decreased. Hard-working kids who learn to look to God for His supernatural provisions also learn to trust Him with their whole lives.

All of our kids worked at least a year between high school and college. Arlyne and I only paid small portions of their college expenses as it was needed. The kids found that God honored their Christian walk, good study habits and diligence as they continued to work their way through college. Their money came primarily through school and summer employment, academic scholarships and grants. But God provided miracles in each semester.

Tim had a great job and was able to take care of his own college expenses. We blessed him with tires for his car and met some of his other needs.

In Elizabeth's case it appeared after her sophomore year that she would be unable financially to return to school. She had worked all summer but didn't have nearly enough. Our family prayed with her for a miracle. Two weeks before ORU began its fall semester God spoke to two couples, one of whom neither Arlyne nor I knew, and told them to pay for her whole semester. Our thrilled daughter returned to school praising the Lord, thankful for His people who listen and obey!

David worked two-and-a-half years after high school. He purchased a fairly new Honda Prelude. The answer to hard work and much prayer, it was his treasure. He kept it spotless. Then God called him to ORU. He gave the car to God, sold it and started school. As a senior he still has not had another car. But he has a great job on campus, and his top grades have earned him a partial scholarship. As resident advisor of his dorm, his room and board are paid for too. Only in his senior year has he taken a very small student loan.

After marrying, Tim wanted a master's degree. He took a student loan then. He is paying fifty dollars a month for ten years and feels the loan was well worth it. But he adds, "I'm sure glad I didn't have to pay for my college years on top of the graduate loan. That would have been a lot more expensive."

Proper Preparation for a Challenging Education

Nothing written in this chapter is meant to keep Christians from getting top educations. But as in the days of Corinth, today most secular community colleges, state colleges and universities are swarming with unhappy, angry professors who appear to know everything but God and His Word. Yet "greater is He who is in [your Christian son or daughter] than he who is in the world" (1 John 4:4, brackets added).

Every Christian has been commanded to "be diligent to present yourself approved to God as a workman who does not need to be ashamed, handling accurately the word of truth" (2 Tim. 2:15). Adequate preparation for advanced learning today requires real answers to this world's philosophies.

David Noebel, director of Summit Ministries, teaches an up-to-the-minute seminar on the latest group-think of both professors and students that your son or daughter will encounter at school. He is extremely well-qualified to present biblical truth to counteract the confusion of secular philosophies. Even if your kids plan to enroll in a Christian school, I would strongly recommend that they attend Summit Ministries for a two-week course prior to entering a junior college, college or university. For full information write: David Noebel, Summit Ministries, Box 207, Manitou Springs, CO 80829; or call (719) 685-9103.

A Person Isn't a Piano Because He Says He Is a Piano!

It is important, when deciding on any Christian elementary to graduate school, to get to know the teachers and professors as much as possible. Any school claiming to be Christian should have excellent Christian teachers with a thoroughly biblical approach to the subjects they teach and a Christ-centered concern for each student. But any supposedly Christian school can have teachers who are as lost as a goose in a blizzard. God's instruction is to "avoid such men as these" (2 Tim. 3:5).

Talk candidly to students who attend. Listen to what your pastor says about the school. Get an honest look at the present spiritual climate of that school or seminary.

Continue to pray about the decision your kids will need to make regarding their education. God will show your family what to do each step of the way.

In your search for riches, don't lose sight of the things money can't buy!

Dear Ray:

Yesterday my daughter was a little girl on a tricycle. Tomorrow she turns sixteen. Time flies when you're having fun! I used to tell her she could date only when she turned forty. But she doesn't seem to like that idea now. So help me with some tips on how to keep this young lady as safe as possible.

I wish she were still on that tricycle!

Papa Needs Answers

Love is patient.
1 Corinthians 13:4a

ELEVEN

WHEN ARE THEY READY TO DATE?

*Since the advent of sex education classes,
the guy who drives the local school bus
can't figure out whether students are
talking dirty or discussing their homework!*

S CHOOL AND DATING — two subjects most people have taken for granted. Yet today's national statistics and the shattered lives of millions in America prove we can't afford to take "pot luck" with either one.

My own book *Singles Plus* is so thorough regarding dating that anything I write in this book to singles or single parents should be followed up by reading it. Not only is it vital for singles of any age, including teenagers, it is also must reading for parents who want to understand their teenagers and help them make the best choices.

197

Your Past Is Past

If you are a Christian parent who once lived a very lost life, you are not a hypocrite for training your kids from the Bible. First John 1:9 has awesome news for you — if you've confessed your sin, you are forgiven — no matter how you lived prior to coming to Christ, the "old things" passed away; "new things have come" (2 Cor. 5:17). This is absolute. A Christian is not the person he or she used to be. Christians simply need to keep on becoming who they are going to be.

It is essential for a Christian parent to realize that no matter how full of sexual sin his or her past life was, it is buried in the deepest sea. God says, "No fishing allowed!" Your past is no reason to soft-pedal the biblical directions for purity that you give to your family. Whether you were moral or immoral, sexual sin must be avoided at all costs by your son or daughter (1 Cor. 6:18-20; Heb. 13:4; Rev. 21:8). Otherwise the price they'll pay for your mistakes will be far too high.

Christian Parents Who Bond

We live in an age that promotes and sells sex. No one — not even little Murgatroid the toddler — can be kept from seeing teeny-weeny polka-dot bikinis and the flesh that oozes from them. But kids who feel good about themselves, know they are deeply loved by their parents and have a close walk with Jesus Christ seldom feel a need to reach outside the home for sex in the name of love. Churchgoing kids often choose sexual sin. But Christ-centered kids, whose parents bond honestly with them, do not want to disappoint their parents — or God.

Teach Your Child About Sex As They Grow

Parents have a deep obligation to teach their children from infancy about God's design for sex. The level of information will need to be increased as the child matures. But the Christian parent must understand how crucial this instruction really is. The government has determined to instruct your child about every possible form of sex beginning in the first grade. And they will usually do so from a very humanistic, antibiblical point of view.

198

You may find it awkward to discuss sex with your child. Concordia Press has created an outstanding series of sex education books for all age levels. You'll find them at your local Christian bookstore.

Puberty

Adolescence is a time when your daughter may tear her pantyhose while hunting Easter eggs. Puberty can be a difficult time for your son or daughter. So prepare yourself; it will happen — and this too shall pass! Puberty usually begins between the ages of ten and fourteen. It is most often signaled by a boy's first nocturnal emission (his first ejaculation, usually in his sleep) or when a girl experiences menarche (the onset of her monthly menstrual cycle).

I recommend that you read Tim and Beverly LaHaye's very helpful book called *Against the Tide*. It covers this subject well.

Preparing for Adolescence by James Dobson is also an excellent book and has an accompanying cassette series. It is intended to aid communication between parent and child on the subject of sexuality. During the midportion of the child's tenth year, I recommend a dad take his son or a mom take her daughter for a daylong, relaxed time of perhaps driving somewhere while listening to Dr. Dobson's tapes followed by discussion. If you are the only parent in the home, you will need to have this conversation with either son or daughter.

After listening to each tape, discuss anything your son or daughter wants to talk about. Be respectful of the fact that they may be embarrassed. Gently lead the conversation. Then let Dr. Dobson teach them. After all the tapes have been played, tell them how you felt as a young person at this age in your own life. Reinforce how important it is to remain free of sex until they marry the man or woman God has chosen for them.

Even though puberty may be years away, it won't be premature to give this information to your ten-year-old. It will help prepare him or her for whenever it comes. Listen to the tapes first so you are prepared for any questions or comments.

The Difficulties of Puberty

Although puberty can begin as early as ten, it is not abnormal for it to delay as late as age sixteen. A teenager's physical changes usually trigger emotional ones as well.

Tragically, at this stage of life self-hatred comes easily for them. Some of the best-looking teenagers don't believe they are. Any acne or extra pounds cause a teenager to feel like a leper. Their peers will often make unkind, sarcastic remarks about these things or cut them out of social activities.

Teenage girls who believe they are unattractive may become anorexic or bulimic in an effort to look slimmer. For specific help for a child or teenager who is not happy with his or her own appearance, read James Dobson's book *Hide and Seek*.

The two groups of adolescents who find the process of puberty most difficult are "early bloomer" girls and "late bloomer" boys.

The early-bloomer girl faces a great deal of problems with her male peers as she is often looked upon as a sex object. Without Christ she is extremely vulnerable. With Christ the temptations will still be strong because nothing in her life experience has prepared her for this new, unwelcomed phenomenon.

The late bloomer may often feel awkward and out of place with peers already experiencing puberty. He knows he's still a "boy" while his peers seem to have turned into "men."

Parents need to minister God's love and hope (Jer. 29:11-13) to kids who feel this way. Encourage your son or daughter in areas where they have gifts and talents. Help them to understand that they have much to contribute right now and that we all have an internal "clock." Let them know their clock is still ticking and will wake them in God's perfect timing.

Why Talk About Sex Before They Have Reached Puberty?

Sex means millions of dollars for everyone from Hollywood moguls to Planned Parenthood. Whether it's a ticket to the latest skin-flick, a cable movie channel or a new client in an abortion clinic, there are megabucks to be made by those who profit from packaged sex. Those making the millions are delighted to produce a steady diet of cheap thrills and immoral activities for anyone they can lure and entrap. What are the results?

- According to the U.S. Centers for Disease Control, 54 percent of all high schoolers have had sexual intercourse, and 69 percent of these are currently sexually active.[1]

- More than half of all girls and almost three-quarters of boys have had sexual intercourse by their eighteenth birthday.[2]

- Of fifteen-year-olds, 4.6 percent were sexually active in 1970. Three out of every ten fifteen-year-olds have had sexual intercourse this year![3]

- Every year three million teenagers acquire a sexually transmitted disease.[4]

- More than one million teenage girls — one in every ten under the age of twenty — become pregnant in the United States every year, and teens have 25 percent of all abortions.[5]

- About 40 percent of all teenage pregnancies now end in abortion. Unmarried teens count for about 97 percent of these...Between 1973 and 1988, the abortion rate for girls ages fourteen and under increased 56 percent...62 percent for those aged fifteen to seventeen...and among older teens, almost 120 percent...In absolute numbers, the youngest group had about 13,000 abortions, the middle group had 158,000, and the oldest group had 234,000...Over 11,000 babies were born to children under the age of fifteen in 1988...Over three million teenagers — one out of six sexually experienced teens — become infected with sexually transmitted diseases each year.[6]

- Twenty percent of AIDS cases occur in people in their twenties — most likely infected as teens.[7]

- Only 26 percent of the men involved in the pregnancies of women under eighteen are that young themselves; 35 percent are eighteen or nineteen; 39 percent are twenty or older.[8]

- Eighty-five percent of teen pregnancies are unintended. Half end in births, a third in abortion, the rest in miscarriage.[9]

- By their early twenties, 71 percent of sexually experienced young women have had more than one partner; 21 percent have had six or more.[10]

- A sizable minority of teens don't have sex; 18 percent are virgins at nineteen.[11]

The U.S. Centers for Disease Control concluded, "The only completely effective means of preventing unintended pregnancy and sexually transmitted diseases is to refrain from sexual intercourse."[12]

Isn't it amazing that, in light of the above statistics, Dr. Joycelyn Elders, the U.S. surgeon general under President Clinton, advocates introducing sex to children at an early age. Dr. Elders told David Brinkley on ABC's "This Week With David Brinkley" that she believes sex education for children should begin at age two.[13]

Nancy Gibbs, writing for *Time* magazine on May 24, 1993, wrote in her cover story, "How Should We Teach Our Children About Sex?":

Just Do It. Just Say No. Just Wear a Condom. When it comes to sex, the message to America's kids is confused and confusing. The moral standards society once generally accepted, or at least paid lip service to, fell victim to the sexual revolution and a medical tragedy. A decade marked by fear of AIDS and furor over society's values made it hard to agree on the ethical issues and emotional context that used to be part of learning about sex. Those on the right reacted to condom giveaways and gay curriculum and throbbing MTV videos as signs of moral breakdown. Those on the left dismissed such concerns as the rantings of religious zealots and shunned almost any discussion of sexual restraint as being reactionary or, worse yet, unsophisticated. "Family values" became a polarizing phrase.

In some sense, the arrival of AIDS in the American psyche a decade ago ended the debate over sex education. Health experts were clear about the crisis...In such a climate of fear, moral debate seemed like a luxury. Get them the information, give them protection, we can talk about morality later. There is a fishbowl full of condoms in the nurse's office, help yourself. While only three states mandated sex ed in 1980, today forty-seven states formally require or recommend it; all fifty support AIDS education.

But as parents and educators watch the fallout from

nearly a decade of lessons geared to disaster prevention — here is a diagram of a female anatomy, this is how you put on a condom — there are signs that this bloodless approach to learning about sex doesn't work. Kids are continuing to try sex at an ever more tender age...twenty-seven percent of fifteen-year-old girls, up from nineteen percent in 1982. Among boys, incidents like the score-keeping Spur Posse gang in California and the sexual-assault convictions of the Glen Ridge, New Jersey, jock stars suggest that whatever is being taught, responsible sexuality isn't being learned.

Condoms and "Safe Sex"

Many teenagers have been told all they need to do to have "safe sex" is use a condom. Schools and other groups are passing condoms out like bubble gum. Yet it is being reported that one in four sexually active teenagers gets a sexually transmitted disease, and one in five sexually active girls gets pregnant.

Condom advertising often changes the term *safe sex* to *safer sex* with condoms. But how much safer do condoms make sex? Obviously, given the above statistics, not safe enough.

Recently a parent asked me, "Does God forbid sexual intercourse if my son uses a condom?" God says, "Flee immorality" (1 Cor. 6:18a), and He forbids sex outside marriage for any reason (Heb. 13:4). In fact, God forbids petting, French kissing and all kinds of physical passion among singles that might easily lead to intercourse. "Now the deeds of the flesh are evident which are: immorality, impurity, sensuality...those who practice such things shall not inherit the kingdom of God" (Gal. 5:19, 21b).

Have you ever been on a diet and stopped to stare through a bakery window at all the goodies you couldn't have? Then you can relate to the desire your kids may have to violate this command from God (see also Eph. 4:17-24; Jude 4).

> Therefore consider the members of your earthly body as dead to immorality, impurity, passion, evil desire, and greed, which amounts to idolatry. For it is on account of these things that the wrath of God will come (Col. 3:5-6).

Is God "the Great Spoilsport"?

God is not Victorian or a spoilsport. God is all loving; He sent Jesus Christ to save each person in this world from an eternal hell (John 3:16). Christ died in your place. And He died for "whosoever will" receive Him as Lord and follow Him. But Christ will never tempt you or your kids (James 1:13) nor lead anyone into sin. He will give you the strength to overcome all temptation (1 Cor. 10:13).

No loving God could ever endorse sexual sin. He sees the heartbreak of the unwed, pregnant daughter and her parents. He understands the agony of the parents who feel they must hurry a son or daughter into a poorly prepared-for marriage. A parent's heart breaks for the teenage girl who feels she must allow her baby to be killed through abortion. Parents weep for the AIDS victim or person full of venereal disease who refused to follow their advice — and live. The guilt, blame, shame and deep emotional pain of sexual immorality are the tools of Satan in the lives of those who participate.

God knows the horrible consequences sexual immorality exacts through AIDS and thirty-eight other sexually transmitted diseases.[14] There are over a hundred million carriers of these diseases in America alone today. Most of these carriers are not "bad" people. They are victims of their own bad choices. Many were urged into immorality by those who felt it was the "normal" thing to do.

Why would God allow AIDS and these other diseases? They are part of the consequences of the sin He forbids humans to commit (Rom. 1:25-27). When we continue to cross God's forbidden boundaries regarding sexual gratification, there is something in our bodies that becomes physically and mentally destructive. AIDS is also the direct result of living in a world full of sin (2 Cor. 4:3-4). God offers salvation to every person through His only begotten Son, even those who have a venereal disease (John 3:16). But He is not responsible for the choices of those who refuse to make Jesus Christ Lord of their lives. He does have authority over every person (Matt. 28:18-20), but He has given each one a free will (Josh. 24:15a) and will bring judgment against those who continually refuse His only begotten Son (John 3:16-21).

God is not duty-bound to stop a venereal disease any more than He is duty-bound to jam His finger in the barrel of a loaded gun if you put it to your temple and pull the trigger.

The Truth About Homosexuality

If you worry whether you gave birth to a child who will "discover" a genetic sexual mis-orientation in his or her teen years, you have been misled. The media and the homosexual lobby have given homosexuals a voice far out of proportion to their numbers. And they don't mind shouting untruths when it serves their aims, as Lou Sheldon, chairman of Traditional Values Coalition, explains:

New research from the liberal Alan Guttmacher Institute published in *Family Planning Perspectives* (March/April 1993) found 2% of males had experienced a homosexual relationship and only 1% had exclusively homosexual relationships....

[The fraud that 10 percent of the population is homosexual] began in 1948 with the Alfred Kinsey Report. Kinsey used data from a sample of interviewees who were unrepresentative of society: a high percentage of prisoners and sex offenders...The Morton-Hunt study for *Playboy* found about 1% of males and .5% of females are homosexual. Homosexual leaders now admit that they knowingly exploited the inaccurate 10% Myth. Tom Stoddard, formerly of the Lambda Legal Defense Fund, told *Newsweek* in February 1993, "We used that figure [10 percent] when most gay people were entirely hidden to try to create an impression of our numerousness."

There is no biological, hormonal or genetically conclusive evidence to substantiate that people are born homosexual. Increasingly, studies from universities such as John Hopkins School of Medicine, Albert Einstein School of Medicine and Masters and Johnson point to environmental factors as major causes. Specifically, a child's perception of family dynamics, a traumatized condition, rape, abuse or other traumatic events may cause gender identity conflict.[15]

Wait to Date

Even before your child is born you need to begin praying for his or her future spouse. Pray: "Lord, give my child the right husband" or "the right wife." Also pray spiritual blessings and protection from God for the one your son or daughter will one day marry. Keep believing God will do these things (Mark 11:24). And don't rush your child or teenager into "boyfriend/girlfriend" relationships.

Sixteen years old is early enough to allow your son or daughter to start dating. Nationwide studies of teenage pregnancies prove the rate of pregnancy among unwed teenage girls is staggeringly higher among teenagers (either male or female) who began dating before the age of sixteen.

Heart Trouble

Any date, even the most casual one, offers a built-in problem:

> The heart is deceitful above all things, and desperately wicked; who can know it? (Jer. 17:9, KJV).

It is an understatement to say you have spent a great deal of time and money raising your son or daughter. The Lord has one goal for your children: to turn them into His winners. If you get any less than that, you'll have had a poor return on your investment!

Far too often a Christian son or daughter ends up marrying someone who is lost. God has stated: "Be ye not unequally yoked together with unbelievers" (2 Cor. 6:14a, KJV).

He goes on to ask: "What has a believer in common with an unbeliever?" (2 Cor. 6:15b).

As a Christian parent, if you want to ensure your children's future happiness, make the following rule. And see that your kids keep it.

Absolutely no dating will be allowed with anyone who does not have Christ at the *center* of his or her life. (Not just any churchgoer will do.)

Why Do You Add "Not Just Any Churchgoer"?

"Just any churchgoer" is not good enough for your son or daughter. So often a teenager drifts into a church with friends. This is as it should be. The teenager may make a momentary decision for Christ in an emotional moment, but instead of becoming a believer he or she becomes a "churchgoer."

Second Corinthians 5:17 never occurs: Old things don't begin to pass away, and scarcely anything in their lifestyle becomes new.

Christ warned of this kind of person in the parable of the seeds (Matt. 13:19-22). To date such a person is spiritually dangerous because he is not committed to Christ and the Christian lifestyle.

Shouldn't I Just Trust the Lord With Whomever My Teenager Dates?

Let's get this straight. You are only obeying God when you enforce 2 Corinthians 6:14 regarding dating. Why did God make the rule? "Do not be deceived. Bad company corrupts good morals" (1 Cor. 15:33).

Never say: "My son or daughter is such an outstanding Christian that it doesn't matter if their date is saved or unsaved. My child's witness for Christ will be enough to change whomever they date."

God answers, "Don't kid yourself!" Our all-wise, all-powerful God knows that good morals won't change bad company; good morals will be corrupted by bad company!

Do You Have the Right to Say No to Certain Date Choices?

If your teenager or young adult is still living in your home, you are his or her spiritual authority (1 Cor. 11:3). If your child chooses to rebel and removes himself or herself from your spiritual covering, he must understand that he will reap the spiritual, emotional and physical consequences of a rebellion. He faces the almost certain possibility of walking in and out of several hurtful relationships; the possibility of a disastrous marriage, a venereal disease or unwanted pregnancy; and wasted years that can never be relived.

An Exception to the Rule

If you are a brand-new Christian and your son or daughter is sixteen or older and has been dating an unsaved person, this rule may be impossible to enforce without seriously damaging your relationship with your teenager. Training children "in the way they should go" is far easier than trying to change them after they are teenagers. It is especially difficult to train older teens in Christian ways if they don't want the Lord in their lives.

Newly saved parents of older teenagers may have to pray diligently and continually, love their teens and try as best they can to share the attractiveness of Christ with them and the ones they are dating. Then trust God for a miracle. Christian parents, however, must never endorse sexual immorality or allow it in their kid's life. Love must be tough at times even if a teenager walks out. The prodigal son walked out, found Christ in a pig pen and came home because his father left the porch light on (Luke 15:11-20).

God's Commands for the Dater

Just before your teenager's first date, do what Arlyne and I did with all the kids we've raised: Have them memorize then recite aloud to you 1 Timothy 4:12:

> Let no one look down on your youthfulness, but rather in speech, conduct, love, faith and purity, show yourself *an example of those who believe* (italics added).

Discuss this verse with them. Be sure they've thought about what each word means and the conduct God expects of them. When your son or daughter meets the qualifications of 1 Timothy 4:12, they are certainly qualified to date if they are sixteen years of age or older.

Remember, dating is cultural, not biblical. Probably most of what your teenager knows about the phenomenon of dating comes from the lifestyles of unsaved peers and the mass media.

Before they even begin dating, spend time teaching your teens appropriate guidelines for a Christian date. Give them ideas and suggestions for activities and behaviors which are pleasing to God. Get my *Singles Plus* book and videos and study them together.

Encourage them to participate in group activities and church functions with their dates.

The Curfew Bell Shall Ring Tonight!

Curfews are absolutely necessary for the safety of the couple and the sanity of the parents. Curfews should be set by considering the length of distance to and from any event, plus a reasonable time for the event. Determine whether you want your teen and date to include one hour afterward for a restaurant stop.

Sometimes having goodies available at your house so that you can chat with your teen and his or her date is a good idea. Just don't leave them alone in your house while you go to bed. Don't lead your son or daughter into temptation!

Your single child is able to have sex in places other than your home, even if they keep a curfew. But nationwide studies prove the number-one place where unmarried teenagers have sex is at one of the parents' homes.[16] In America, a teenage girl becomes pregnant nearly every thirty seconds.[17] Don't let it happen in your home.

Be careful what words you say to your teenagers if they ever come home late from a date. Set the discipline *before* such a thing occurs. Then you won't be tempted to think of progressively worse things to do to them as the minutes tick away!

Remember: If you only let your kids date Christians who have placed Christ at the center of their lives, you have far less to worry about. Cars do run out of gas or have flat tires, but not every night!

Trust Has to Be Earned

Trust doesn't come automatically, just because someone was born in your home and reached a particular age. Trust has to be earned. Provide more and more responsibility as your teenagers grow from puberty to adulthood. In this way they can prove that they have become increasingly trustworthy. Always try to help them stay away from temptation. Praise them every time they succeed.

Can a Young Person Remain a Virgin Until Marriage?

Millions of people throughout history have had happy, healthy, long lives and died virgins at ripe old ages. Sex is not a biological necessity like breathing, eating or sleeping.

God created us as sexual beings and gave us a sex drive. But He also gave us the power to control that sex drive until marriage.

Single people can know, without doubt, that they are in full charge of their own sexuality and have kept their sex drive under God's full control. They can also know that the one they choose to marry is also in charge of *his or her* sex drive. Thus, they can marry with the greatest assurance that neither they nor their spouse will ever destroy the marriage and family through sexual immorality.

Trust is an absolute necessity in marriage. A teenager or single person who had sex before marriage is totally untrustworthy as a marriage partner. When a couple (especially a Christian couple) violates the Lord's command (Heb. 13:4), they are declaring to each other that neither can be trusted in marriage.

What if one should be sent overseas by the military or the company for which he or she works for a period of time? Suppose, by necessity, they had to be gone for a year or two. How could the one, knowing the other person had been totally willing to sin against God through immorality (Gen. 39:9; Job 31:1; Ps. 51:4), ever believe that person *wouldn't* violate their marriage covenant by having sex with someone else? And how could the one overseas morally trust the one who stayed home? The lack of trust obviously would be a strong destructive factor in the marriage. So God commands abstinence before marriage.

She Told It Like It Is

A lovely single girl who was hurried into an abortion before she came to Christ told me,

> I was graduating as a senior from high school, and all my girlfriends told me about their sexual experiences. I thought something was wrong with me because I'd never done it. So I went out with a football player and gave my virginity away. In five minutes of pain I found out it wasn't what I'd been told at all. I felt dirty afterward and threw up.
>
> The guy never even dated me after that night. But then I found I was pregnant. I didn't know the Lord. My parents were so hurt and mad and told me to get rid of the baby. Dad even drove me to get my abortion and sat in the car all the time it was happening. I thought the physical pain alone would kill me. Then I saw something that must have been a piece of the baby. I screamed and screamed. I still have nightmares over that.
>
> Afterward I staggered back to the car. My dad said, "Well, that's done." But it wasn't. That kind of thing never is. Even though I know the Lord now and am washed in Christ's blood, I have that memory. And the devil sure is

the tormentor. I wish I could tell every single, *please* don't be a fool and have sex before marriage.

Spiritual Virginity

Young people who have already fallen into sexual sin need to realize God can still restore them to wholeness. In 1 John 1:9 God not only promises to "forgive" the sinner, but to "cleanse them from all unrighteousness." The Greek word for "cleanse" means "to restore totally." Christ "cleansed" lepers. He didn't "heal" them. Lepers were not left with any missing parts that had vanished because of the leprosy. Everything was restored as though they had never been lepers, just as the ear Peter cut off was totally restored in wholeness to the Roman soldier (Luke 22:49-51). Honest confession to Christ and a repentance from former immorality brings total spiritual cleansing and restored spiritual virginity (1 Cor. 6:9-11).

Christian Young People Are Giving Their Bodies to God

And so, dear brothers, I plead with you to give your bodies to God. Let them be a living sacrifice, holy — the kind He can accept. When you think of what He has done for you, is this too much to ask? Don't copy the behavior and customs of this world, but be a new and different person with a fresh newness in all you do and think. Then you will learn from your own experience how His ways will really satisfy you (Rom. 12:1-2, TLB).

True Love Waits is a movement spearheaded by the Southern Baptists and now joined by many other denominations and Christian organizations in the United States and dozens of foreign countries. It recruits singles, including teenagers, to sign a covenant to stay pure before the Lord until they give their bodies to their husbands or wives. Thousands of young people are taking this pledge. For more information about True Love Waits, write to True Love Waits, 127 Ninth Ave. N., Nashville, TN 37234, or call toll-free 1-800-LUVWAIT.

A Lit Lantern

When our daughter, Elizabeth, made plans to become Mrs. Todd

Hinson, I was surprised to hear her say that she didn't intend to carry the traditional bridal bouquet — she planned to carry a lit lantern. She explained, "Todd was reading about the five wise virgins and the five foolish virgins in Matthew 25:1-11. Then he had a dream about them. The wise virgins were able to light their lamps. So when I walk down the aisle on our wedding day, we want to let everyone in the church know Todd is marrying a virgin."

Arlyne found a beautiful antique lantern. And on the day of Elizabeth and Todd's wedding, the Rev. Tim Mossholder performed the ceremony that united them. David Mossholder sang to the bride and groom. And this proud papa walked down that aisle with a beautiful bride who was announcing to the world that she had been faithful to her covenant with Christ throughout all her single days. Praise the Lord!

The Single's Covenant of Abstinence

At the close of each Singles Plus seminar, the singles commit themselves to the Lord's call of abstinence until marriage. I offer this simple but profound pledge to all parents who want to conclude their key talk by leading their single son or daughter to make this vow to Christ:

Lord, I am willing never to be married. I will care about every person I date, and they will only be members of the opposite sex who deeply love You too. But from this moment on I promise You I will be a *virgin* until I am married. Thank You for giving me the power to keep this commitment. In Jesus' name. Amen.

**When we really live for the approval
of God, we don't have to worry at all
about the approval of others.**

212

Dear Ray:

Sweden and my kids believe spankings should be outlawed. In fact, my eight- and twelve-year-olds seem to be against every form of discipline. We love our kids. We don't want to raise juvenile delinquents. Nor do we want to harm them psychologically and scar them forever. What's a parent to do about discipline?

A Dad And Mom Who Want
Someday to Spend Eternity
in Heaven With Our Kids

Don't you realize that you can choose
your own master? You can choose sin
(with death) or else obedience (with
acquittal). The one to whom you offer
yourself — he will take you and be your
master and you will be his slave.
Thank God that though you once chose
to be slaves of sin, now you have
obeyed with all your heart the teaching
to which God has committed you.
And now you are free from your old
master, sin; and you have become slaves
to your new master, righteousness.
Romans 6:16-18, TLB

TWELVE

KIDS NEED TO KNOW THE RULES

*When parents don't mind
that their children don't mind,
the children don't mind.*

IMAGINE TURNING ON the radio to listen to your favorite team play football and hearing the announcer say, "Jones has the ball on the forty-yard line. He hands it to Smith. Smith takes it to the thirty. To the twenty. To the ten. To the twenty. To the thirty. To the twenty. To the thirty!" What is wrong with Smith? He has no *goal!*

Just as confused as the above football player is the family without goals or a game plan for life. When one doesn't know where he is going he can make a very loud bump! A broken nose is very painful. A broken life is even more painful.

Kids need limits. They must know exactly what those limits are. The story is told of a doctor who was examining a woman while her little four-year-old was opening the bottles of medicine on the doctor's shelf. "I hope you don't mind Bobo's curiosity, doctor," the woman said. "He just likes to investigate everything."

"Oh, I don't mind," the doctor replied. "If he takes just one of those pills he's poured into his hand, he'll be very quiet for the rest of his life!"

You aren't helping your children by letting them grow wild and "free." Without absolute rules that are always kept; boundaries that you will never let your kid cross without definite consequences; principles and guidelines you enforce until they become natural for them, you do great harm to them. Jesus Christ is the way, the truth and the life, and no one gets to the Father except through Him (see John 14:6). Let them drive the wrong way on the freeway, and you will lose your kids. From babyhood on, they have to learn which way to go.

Three Rules About Rules

Wise parents will make rules for each child, teenager or single adult in their home. Any rule will have these three qualifications:

1. Each rule will be given in order to protect the kids' spirits, souls and/or bodies. It will also be set to keep a parent from worry.

2. Clear boundaries (limits) will be set. The parents will tell the kids what they can and can't do.

3. Breaking any rule will be dealt with consistently and lovingly by parental discipline.

Why Discipline Your Kids?

The six-year-old "puffed away" on a chocolate cigarette as her mom and dad laughed. Her dad said, "She is so cute when she's being naughty." I wondered how long it would be before he would regret that statement.

Naughtiness is never cute to God. Naughtiness is the first step of sin. Sin leads to death (Rom. 6:23a).

To keep kids from physical or spiritual death, parents have to teach them that the word *No!* is a complete sentence. No is the first discipline your child should learn. Yes and no are the limit-setting words that create rules in a family.

Parents have to be consistent with discipline. Kids must know you mean what you say.

The root of the word *discipline* is "disciple." We are to disciple our kids into a lifestyle of being Christ's disciple (John 8:31-32). It will require the same kind of persistence that Jesus used in training His twelve disciples.

Parents who keep firm guidelines and let their kids know they are loved almost always raise well-balanced Christian kids. Kids raised this way are extremely likeable. They are comfortable in a crowd or one-on-one. They can be trusted to tell the truth.

Setting Boundaries

Little Ignatz can walk into walls or fall out of second-story windows if you let him. Or he can stay safe and secure within the boundaries you set as a parent. The same is true of your teenage daughter Paprika. If you love your kids you will set boundaries and hold them responsible to stay within them. Setting boundaries does not mean being tightly rigid — the more Christlike, responsible and trustworthy the kids become, the wider the boundaries can be set.

Your prayers, Christlike actions, hugs and love will reinforce that you deeply care about them. It will show them how life works best — with rules. They will be safe in a world where others are wandering over cliffs. Discipline doesn't break a child's spirit half as much as the lack of it breaks a parent's heart!

Punishment or Discipline?

Bibles translated into English from their original texts often miss the heart of God in not separating the meanings of punishment and discipline. But any careful reading of God's Word clearly demonstrates the difference over and over again.

Death-row sentences, life imprisonment, hell and any form of torture are forms of *punishment.* Punishment is given to someone who is undesirable and too dangerous to live with the general population. They must be separated permanently, or at least for a while, from nonviolent, law-abiding people.

Punishment is something some parents do *to* their kids in order to vent their own parental wrath. Usually it will turn the kids into emotionally scarred adults.

Discipline is something parents do *for* their kids. It enforces a consequence that, though temporary, is undesired by any kid. The kids will thus learn that certain forbidden actions bring unpleasant consequences. Christian parents can thereby help their children to learn to make right choices and grow into emotionally healthy adults.

Many Kids Are Self-Destructing

A lack of discipline is evident in our world today. The baby boomers and flower children of the 1970s who wanted their children and themselves to be totally free of moral or any other restraints have raised a generation of kids out of control.

Read any newspaper or watch any newscast and you'll hear the tragic reports of what is happening to millions of kids as they self-destruct. The following is just a tip of the iceberg:

> Arrests of people under age eighteen for violent crime rose 47 percent from 1988 to 1992. One in six arrests for murder, rape, robbery or assault is of a suspect under age eighteen. Slayings by teenagers rose by 124 percent from 1986 to 1991. In 1992, young people killed 3,400 people nationwide.[1]

Eight of every ten deaths among adolescents are violent, making them the number-one victims of premature death.[2] Suicide rates for young people aged fifteen to nineteen quadrupled from 1950 to 1991. In 1990, 276,000 high school students in the United States made at least one suicide attempt requiring medical attention.[3]

More than 70 percent of teen suicides are from broken homes. In 1990, guns were involved in one in four deaths of young people aged fifteen to twenty-four. Guns now account for 39 percent more deaths of teenagers than disease does. Among ages fifteen to nineteen, only motor vehicle fatalities take more of their lives than guns do.[4]

There are three signs that may indicate a teenager is contemplating suicide:

1. Behavior: Any sudden, unexpected change may signal suicidal thinking, such as failing grades, isolation from activities and associations, changes in eating or sleeping habits, extreme irritability and reckless, defiant or physically aggressive behaviors.

2. Verbal: These clues may be either direct or indirect, such as, "What would you say if I were to kill myself?" "Everyone would be better off without me" or "You won't have to worry about me much longer."

3. Life experiences: These are external conditions over which the teenager has no control. They include any feelings of great loss and deep sorrow. "Let every person be in subjection to the governing authorities" (Rom. 13:1). If your young person (or anyone you love) begins to exhibit any of the above symptoms, get Christian counseling help immediately. With suicide threats, the law also requires notification of the police, who are trained to deal with the situation. Anyone talking about killing himself or herself nearly always means it.

Alcoholic Teenagers

Before a child reaches drinking age, he or she will have seen alcohol being consumed on television seventy-five thousand times and watched it advertised as fun, delicious, attractive and what mature people do. Nine in ten high school seniors have experimented with alcohol. Every two weeks an estimated 40 percent of them consume five or more drinks in one sitting.[5] Of tenth graders, 21.1 percent, and 13.4 percent of eighth graders also consume five or more drinks in one sitting at least every two weeks.[6] Of college students, 86 percent drink alcohol sometime during the year — 45 percent say they drink at least weekly.[7]

Much More Than Aspirin

In 1993, 9.2 percent of eighth graders, 19.2 percent of tenth graders and 21.9 percent of high school seniors had smoked marijuana. Of eighth graders, 11 percent had tried inhalants. At all high school grade levels 17 percent had used inhalants sometimes during the year. Cigarette use among students was on the rise.[8]

Drug abuse is prevalent among teenagers. One study reports that over half of high school seniors have tried marijuana, with 5 percent using it daily.

Other "harder" drugs are far less prevalent among teenagers, though far too often killing many. However, harder drugs aren't required to destroy a life. Marijuana can do it easily.

Youth evangelist Tom Alexander is the founder of Teen Scene in Bakersfield, California, a Christ-centered, drop-in recreation youth center where children and teenagers can have fun and discover the love of Christ. Tom is an excellent counselor of teens, and, because of the epidemic of marijuana usage among the young, he continually gleans every week's report from the National Institution of Drug Abuse in Rockville, Maryland. Recently Tom wrote to me, sharing the truth about marijuana.

Today's marijuana contains THC (tetrahydracannibol), which is ten times more potent than twenty years ago, making it far more destructive to the human body. This marijuana damages chromosomes and also does DNA damage in humans. Marijuana alters the female menstrual cycle and adversely affects the female reproductive tract. Many more miscarriages occur to marijuana-using females than to those who do not smoke it. Meanwhile, male users produce a greater number of abnormally shaped sperm and have a lower sperm count.

Marijuana damages the respiratory system, including lung tissue. Marijuana also damages the immune system, including white blood cells, which fight all sickness and infections. One marijuana cigarette (joint) contains sixteen times more cancer-causing tars and carcinogens than a tobacco-filled cigarette. Animals develop cancer from even moderate use.

THC destroys or damages brain cells and brain tissue, resulting in amotivational syndrome, a feeling of emotional flatness, indifference and the inability or non-desire to compete in life. This increased confusion in thinking, impaired judgment, passivity (zombie-likeness) and hostility toward authority.

Marijuana is fat-soluble, which means it stays in the body long after the initial intoxicative "high" is gone. THC remains in the body's fatty organs (the brain and sex organs) for up to thirty days. Hence, the danger to the brain and reproductive systems. Other "harder" drugs are far less prevalent among teenagers, though far too often killing many. However, harder drugs aren't required to destroy a life. Marijuana can do it easily. Marijuana is death on the installment plan — the grim "reefer" of drugs.[9]

A nation of marijuana smokers would be a nation any anti-Christ dictator could easily own and operate.

Suicide announcements, alcoholism and drug addiction need more than a Band-Aid approach from Christian parents.

> Brethren, even if a [person] is caught in any trespass, you who are spiritual, restore such a one in a spirit of gentleness; looking to yourself, lest you too be tempted (Gal. 6:1).

This is no time for a "How could you do this to me?" kind of self-pity. Professional Christian help may be expensive, but it can save your loved one's life. Tough love is vital at such a time as this. Seek your pastor's counsel.

Teenage Gangs

On a certain night in April 1993, most of the people were missing at the little church in the heart of Bridgeport's ghetto where I was holding a Marriage Plus seminar. They were at a funeral.

On the previous Sunday morning when I began the seminar, a

mother who had come to learn more about family life returned home after church to see a young man enter her home and point a gun at her seventeen-year-old son.

"I pleaded with him," she later told her pastor, Nathaniel Hayes. "Please don't kill my boy!" But he wouldn't listen. Instead, he pumped twenty-three bullets into her son.

Hundreds attended the funeral. Every overflow room in the large funeral parlor was filled with rival ethnic gangs. A couple of hundred more stood outside and listened by loudspeaker. One young man after another stood to read an original poem — all on the theme of revenge.

Three girls sat near the casket weeping. Each one had mothered one of the dead boy's babies.

What was the reason for this murder? The boy now dead had danced with his killer's girlfriend the week before. Pastor Hayes says this kind of incident causes murders "many times a week."

At the funeral Pastor Hayes gave the eulogy and stressed the urgency to receive Christ. Several hands were raised indicating a desire for salvation. But bitterness keeps a heart from really being transformed by Christ (Matt. 6:14-15). So the murdering continues.

Good-bye, Dad and Mom

Nearly one million young people run away or are thrown out of their homes every year. They come from every socioeconomic, ethnic and racial group. One in three is lured into prostitution within forty-eight hours.

Runaway kids leave home of their own accord, often fleeing deplorable situations. The average age of runaways is fifteen or under. Seventy-five percent of these are from single-parent homes. One in four was born to mothers under the age of eighteen. More than 80 percent run away for the first time within three hundred miles of their home.

Throwaway kids are forced out of their homes by families who are either unable or unwilling to take responsibility for them any longer. Some have never cared for them at all. The average age of throwaway boys is seventeen, girls fifteen. Over half come from single-parent homes and/or from homes where one or both parents are alcoholics. At least half report having been physically or sexually abused by parents.[10]

Laura Myers, a writer for the Associated Press, reported the results of one of the most extensive studies ever done among throwaway kids. Stanford University for the Center of Families, Children and Youth conducted an extensive, two-year project. One teenager who was interviewed said: "It is cold and miserable on the streets, but it is better than being beaten up by parents who don't care." Fifty-two percent of throwaway teens stay on the streets, refusing help because they are afraid they'll be sent back home.[11]

Accidents, murders and suicides (in that order) are more responsible for keeping young people from reaching the age of twenty-five than disease is. Eight of ten deaths among adolescents and young adults are violent, making them the number-one victims of premature death.

One street kid said:

Everyone has a dream of a family and a decent place to live, but only a few of us will ever have it. One third of us will be killed before we're thirty. Another third will be in mental institutions or prisons. The other third will slit their wrists...It's like realizing you can't wake up from a nightmare...You escape to the streets and you figure you're a big hit. Then you don't want to be a hit anymore. You want to be a simple little kid again.

Arise, cry aloud in the night
At the beginning of the night watches;
Pour out your heart like water
Before the presence of the Lord;
Lift up your hands to Him
For the life of your little ones
Who are faint because of hunger
At the head of every street (Lam. 2:19).

The Buddy System

Do not be deceived: "Bad company corrupts good morals" (1 Cor. 15:33).

This verse warns us to beware of making bad choices when we develop close friendships.

A few years ago I was driving to a meeting at a church in Southern California when I turned on the car radio and found a station playing twenty-four hours of old-time radio. These were the kinds of programs I'd spent my childhood listening to with my mom: clean and hilarious comedy programs like Fibber McGee and Molly, Baby Snooks, Edgar Bergen and Charlie McCarthy. Suddenly I burst into tears. I pulled the car to the side of the road and stopped. I couldn't believe I was crying. I hardly ever cry. For a moment I thought, I'm cracking up! But then I realized why I was crying. My favorite childhood friends were saying hello and making me laugh again. I had missed them so much!

If my childhood radio "friends" had such a profound effect on me, how much more do our living friends influence and affect our intellect, emotions and will? Teach your children that they will have many *acquaintances*. But to choose a friend is to choose a major impact on their lives. It's not just in marriage that people affect you for better or for worse. Close friends do that too. That's why you can't afford to have your kid choose wrong friends, those that will influence them for the worse.

Everyone should try to like everyone else. Loving Christians can always win friends and influence people for Christ. But both your kids and your best friends should always be deeply committed Christians. Enforce that kind of choosing with your kid at every age level. You have that right as a parent. Of course, you'll have to really know their closest friends to do that. Encourage your kid to welcome their best friends to come to your house often, add them to outings with your family, enjoy them. One of the biggest reasons my kids love Christ so much as adults is because their closest friends as kids did too.

Feeding the Mind "a Different Gospel"

The people on the talk shows and the dialogue on the sitcoms being broadcast over television today generally make a poor choice of "friends." These programs prove this is a very sick society in which we live. Those who watch most of these programs regularly tend to get caught up in their humanistic and hedonistic philosophies. Most programs could rightly flash a sign as they begin: Warning: This program may be hazardous to your mental health.

Christ can't work *through* you unless He is given time to work *in* you. If you want your walk with Him to last, you have to put Him first.

I challenge you to lead your family in a one-month television fast. Except for an hour of Christian television daily, keep the TV set turned off for one whole month. By doing that you can wean yourself from anything you or the rest of your family is watching that is questionable. Meanwhile, take the time normally spent on TV and develop some family fun. Play some games, spend fifteen minutes in prayer together, read the Bible and renew your family's minds (Rom. 12:2).

Two Mighty Promises From the Lord

It would be easy for a Christian parent to despair at the tremendous responsibility of raising a child in today's world. But the Word of God has given parents two magnificent promises. If disciplining your child is something new to you, lay claim to these promises. Hang them on a wall in your home so you can see and remember them:

Discipline your son and he will give you happiness and peace of mind (Prov. 29:17, TLB). (Throughout Proverbs, the word *son* usually stands for son or daughter.)

All discipline for the moment seems not to be joyful, but sorrowful; yet to those who have been trained by it, afterwards it yields the peaceful fruit of righteousness (Heb. 12:11).

The Parents' Roles in Discipline

The two promises above make it perfectly clear that Christian parents have no other option than to discipline their children. God has ordained that role, and if we do our part — discipline — He will do His part — and will guide us every step of the way.

The Bible states clearly:

And fathers...bring [your children] up in...discipline (Eph. 6:4).

God has assigned the father in each family the role of disciplinarian. The book of Hebrews expands on this responsibility:

> Furthermore, we had earthly fathers to discipline us, and we respected them...For they disciplined us for a short time as seemed best to them (Heb. 12:9a, 10a).

These verses give hope to fathers who wonder if they can be successful in the role of disciplinarian. God simply says, "Your dads did it the best way they knew, and you still respect them, don't you?"

It is the dads who do not discipline their kids who lose the respect of God and their family. An undisciplined son or daughter will make you wish you could disown him or her:

> For those whom the Lord loves He disciplines, and He scourges every son whom He receives. It is for discipline that you endure; God deals with you as with sons; for what son is there whom his father does not discipline? But if you are without discipline, of which all have become partakers, then you are illegitimate children and not sons (Heb. 12:6-8).

A mom shares the responsibility to provide discipline to her children:

> The rod and reproof give wisdom,
> But a child who gets his own way brings shame to his
>   mother (Prov. 29:15).

An undisciplined child will be an embarrassment to his mother even as an adult. If a dad absolutely refuses to discipline his own children, the mom will have to do it. But God will hold the father responsible for not doing it. Mothers are also to provide discipline when needed if Dad isn't home or is in another room when *kid-rebellion* takes place.

In the remaining pages of this chapter I want to help you

discover some appropriate ways to discipline. We will also look at some inappropriate discipline as we discover principles to help raise our children to serve God.

Consequences Motivate

The following principle is one of the most important things for you to remember as you begin to discipline: *Any discipline not interpreted by the receiver as an appropriate consequence for their wrongdoing will not help them to change. It may actually intensify further wrong actions.*

As I sat waiting for an airplane at the Los Angeles airport, a woman sat down next to me with her five-year-old daughter. The young girl wriggled in and out of her chair. Suddenly the woman screamed, "If you don't stop squirming, I'm going to get on that airplane today and leave you here!"

Instantly the terrified girl began pleading with her mother, "No, Mommy. No! I'll be good. Please don't leave me again." I knew by her terror and the sound of her voice when she said "again" that this wasn't the first time her mother had threatened to leave her — nor the first time she had left. The mother's threat worked — the little girl stopped squirming.

That five-year-old girl did not have the maturity to think to herself, This is an inappropriate response to my squirming. But by the time she's a teenager, under the same circumstances she would most likely scream back at her mother, "Who cares? Take the stupid plane. Who needs you anyway?"

Beauty in Ashes

The high school senior girl seemed to have it all — beauty, talent and popularity. And she'd just been voted homecoming queen. The thrill she felt was beyond belief. That night on the phone she shared her tremendous joy with her closest girlfriend. Just before making the call, she had stacked the dishes in the dishwasher but had forgotten to turn it on. Her sweater was draped on the couch nearby.

As she talked, her mother noticed both oversights and told her father. Suddenly her father grabbed the phone out of her hand and hung it up. "Now, Miss Fancypants," he blurted out, "we are going to have a talk. Who in the blue blazes do you think you are? You waltz into this house, eat your Mom's delicious cooking and don't even wash the dishes. You throw your clothes all over the house as though you were the queen of Sheba!"

Stunned, the girl tried to apologize. "I'm sorry, Dad. In the excitement I forgot."

With an expression of victory on his face, her dad replied, "I'll just have to help you remember better. Tomorrow you will march back down to your school and tell them you *cannot* be homecoming queen — and that's final!" As the girl pleaded with him, he turned around haughtily and walked out of the room.

He would not change his mind even when the principal of the high school phoned the next day. Finally it was announced to the entire student body that she could not be homecoming queen. The girl grew bitter, and only the love of Jesus could change her now.

She knew her father's response to the unwashed dishes and carelessly tossed sweater was totally inappropriate. Yes, both should have been attended to before phoning her friend. But she had been humiliated before the entire student body over a minor infraction of family rules. The high honor and responsibility she had been given by the student body had been stolen away in a moment of anger. Made bitter through this humiliation, she now believes neither of her parents really loves or cares about her.

Let me ask you: When the mother threatened her young daughter at the airport or the father humiliated his daughter for her careless mistakes, who needed the greater lesson in discipline — the child or the parent? I think you'll agree in both situations it was the parent.

The Parent, God and Discipline

The way you handle discipline will teach your kids their first lessons about God. Will they see God as:

- A stern, angry God.

- A negative, griping God.

- A God who warns but seldom means it.

- Or a God of love who disciplines us because He loves us (Heb. 12:6, 10b).

Proper discipline fits the "crime." For example, if your child has been warned not to play baseball near a window and then breaks the window, have him earn the money and pay for a new window. A spanking won't get the window repaired! Inappropriate discipline will only serve to drive your child away from you — and in many cases, from God.

Unfair Discipline

Unfair discipline may take several forms. Be careful to avoid the following forms of discipline:

1. Inconsistent discipline; disciplining only when you're angry or in the mood to discipline.

2. Rude, sarcastic or biting comments that humiliate your kids or cause them to hate you.

3. Disciplining one child for an offense for which you did not discipline another.

4. Disciplining kids for something they did not know was wrong or for an honest mistake.

5. Punishing rather than disciplining them. (See the definitions of both these terms on pages 5-6 of this chapter.)

Ineffective Discipline

The following forms of discipline will work about as well with your kids as a screen door at the bottom of a submarine:

No Carry Through
Kids quickly lose respect for the parent who threatens but does not carry out the threat. If you say, "If you don't do so-and-so, I'm going to...," be sure you have spoken fairly. Then do as you've stated. Don't threaten; discipline!

Don't give an order and get so absorbed in something else that you forget to see your order carried out. Never make a rule unless you use proper discipline every time it is broken. Don't nag; train!

Life Sentences

You live in a home, not a prison. A year of grounding is far too extreme. Even a month is too long unless the child or teenager is being disciplined for illegal activity. If you are going to ground your kids, be sure the length of time you ground them is appropriate. A day or a weekend will probably be enough. Grounding takes careful supervision.

Curtail their pleasurable activities: no getting together with friends either by phone or in person; also no TV, radio, cassettes or CDs (unless it is Christian music), driving privileges, going out — whatever they wish they could do. Meanwhile, increase their chores at home. Just remember: The objective is to get their attention and change their behavior because you love them — they're not to be treated as outcasts.

Take into account the age of your child. A preschooler can be disciplined effectively by having him or her sit in a corner with hands folded for three minutes!

The Countdown

There are parents who count for little Horatio or Suzudoo: "1...2...3!" If you are teaching your child to count — wonderful! But when was the last time you heard God lean down from heaven and say: "1...2...3"? God urges parents to use consistent, immediate discipline when their children break any rule they know they shouldn't break.

Children know how far Mommy or Daddy will count before they act and will therefore move just before the anticipated last number.

Be sure you have first fully explained the behavior you will accept and the consequences if not obeyed. Never say, "If you do that *again*...!" If they did it once, they did it. Discipline them.

If you have been using the counting method, tell your kids you are sorry and ask them to forgive you. God loves each of us and wants us to obey Him quickly so that He can bless us. Tell your kids you now realize God wants parents to discipline their children and teenagers for the very same reasons, and from now on there will be no more counting. You will expect them to obey you the first time you speak. But give them one week of grace while you and they are learning to do things God's better way.

Sometimes mere words are not enough — discipline is needed. For the words may not be heeded (Prov. 29:19, TLB).

Learning Appropriate Discipline

It is possible to administer consistent, biblical discipline which will train your kids well. In this section we will consider some principles of godly discipline.

Teenage Discipline: Remove Pleasures — Not Responsibilities

As I've already stated, cancel the pleasurable activities. In addition to removing their pleasures, increase their responsibilities. Add chores, have them do the dishes for a week, wash the windows or mow the lawn every week for a month.

Don't cancel a date you have already approved. Keep your word. Unless their preplanned date has helped to cause the problem, your teenager has a responsibility to keep that date. Otherwise you are punishing your kid's date.

Don't cancel your son or daughter's part in an athletic event, a school play or any rehearsals for these. If your child is being coached (and this includes Little League), they are being counted on by the coach and the team.

Never tell them they have to stay home from church because of what they have done. They need to be there. The church is the most powerful influence your child has besides you.

Spankings

Spankings can fall under the category of either *punishment* or *discipline*, depending on how they are given. If given in a punishing form by an angry parent who is lashing out without self-control, spankings can harm a person both physically and emotionally for a lifetime.

Spankings are intended for children, not teenagers. The older a child grows, the less he should require spankings. There are far better ways to discipline teenagers.

Because the subject of spanking has become such a volatile issue in today's world, we will take a careful look at it on the following pages.

Parent: Discipline Yourself

Discipline your son while there is hope, but do not [indulge your angry resentments by undue chastisements and] set yourself to his ruin (Prov. 19:18, AMP).

Hideous things have been done to kids as punishment. Four out of five convicts in prison were abused kids, not *disciplined* kids. Nearly all of these tragic situations arose from homes with drunken, drugged or neurotic parents who had lost complete charge of their emotions.

Parents must be in control of themselves during any form of discipline. Never wait until you erupt in anger. You may be righteously angry over something your child has done, but discipline your child only to help your child — never to get even. Otherwise they will learn to fear your emotions and not listen to your counsel. The right reason for *any form* of discipline is to change the child's will from a desire to do wrong to a desire to do right.

Administer spankings with "I love you. That's why I'm not going to let you get away with this behavior." *Not* "You little brat! I'm going to whip the tar out of you."

If you are a parent who can bring yourself to spank only when you are "mad enough," I discourage you from ever spanking. Instead consider more creative forms of discipline. God never intended for you to beat your child. No parent has a "right" to abuse a child any more than any child has a right to "abuse" a parent. There were three million reported cases of child abuse in America in 1993, and thirteen hundred of these cases resulted in the death of the youngster.

Brutal beatings, violent shakings (that can often cause severe physical as well as emotional damage), biting, strangling, eye gouging, suffocating, burning, poisoning, constant criticizing, belittling, insulting, sexual advances or involvement, starving and parent abandonment are against the law of human decency — and against God's law. Children must be protected from all forms of punishment.

The Word *Rod* in the Book of Proverbs

The Hebrew word for "rod" means "a stick, or a neutral object." Proverbs links discipline for children with the word *rod*. Since the rod is "a neutral object," do not use your hand to spank your child. Don't cause them to be afraid of your hand. The Bible always speaks of the laying on of hands for blessings. Never slap your child.

> Do not hold back discipline from the child,
> Although you beat [spank] him with the rod, he will
>   not die (Prov. 23:13, brackets added).

Granted, a kid may *act* as though he is going to die! Some children are real Academy Award winners when it comes to getting a spanking. My son David, at the age of seven, loved to be in a room with mirrors when he was spanked. That way he could watch himself cry afterward!

> You shall beat him with the rod,
> And deliver his soul from Sheol [hell] (Prov. 23:14).

How to Give a Spanking in Jesus' Name

What is a godly spanking? Here are the ten steps:

1. Take the child to a private place away from anyone else to avoid being shamed in front of other people.

2. Have your children tell you why they are being spanked. Ask them, "Which rule have you just broken?" Remind them if they don't give you the answer.

3. Have your children put their hands in a safe place — on their knees or on the edge of a bathtub or bed. If this is new for them, tell them, "I love you, and though you are going to get a spanking, you won't be injured." A child trying to get away from a rod can twist his body in such an awkward way as to receive a blow in the face or the eye or some other place that should not be struck. Never let that happen.

4. Spank your children and bring pain. Proverbs 20:30 says, "Punishment [discipline] that hurts chases evil

from the heart" (TLB). Be sure to have a rod that will pack a punch and fits the bottom. Don't use a rod too big for a little child or too little for a big child. Rods come in the form of wooden spoons, paddles or any item that will sting but never maim. (Maybe you should use a Tupperware spoon. If it breaks, they will give you a new one free!)

5. Spank enough, but don't overdo it. Usually children will be disciplined sufficiently with one to three swats.

6. Reassure your children. Tell them you love them too much to let them develop a habit that would make them unhappy for a lifetime. Remind them the spanking was done only to help them stop this bad habit.

7. Forgive your children. After they have apologized for being wrong, look them directly in the eyes and tell them, "I love you, and I forgive you."

8. Kneel down with your children and have them ask the Lord for His forgiveness. Scripture promises us, "If we confess our sins, He is faithful and just to forgive us our sins and to cleanse us from all un-righteousness" (1 John 1:9, KJV).

9. Be sure your children make restitution. For example, if one of your children has hit another and you have spanked him for doing it, watch him as he goes out to apologize to the one he hit. If he is rude rather than apologetic, call him back and give him the same number of swats again. Why? Because in step 8 he lied to God!

10. Once your children have repented, never mention the incident again. Aren't you glad Psalm 103:12 tells you that God will remove your sins "as far as the east is from the west" when you confess them? Do the same for your children. Every time they break a rule is the *first* time, because they've been forgiven for their past failures.

What Kind of a Dad Are *You,* Ray?

When David was a junior in high school, he wrote a letter rich with insight into how a teenager feels about a delayed consequence.

For several days David had been leaving our home late for his first morning class at his high school. Both Arlyne and I were deeply concerned that he could be hurt in an accident on his wild dash for class. We also knew he was getting into trouble with his teacher because of his late arrivals. I had threatened to ground him several days that week but hadn't done so. The morning I finally did ground him, David responded by saying, "I don't love you anymore!" This compounded his sentence. That night I found this letter from David shoved under my bedroom door:

Dear Dad:

I reacted the way I did when you told me I was grounded because I was angry. I got upset, and I said something I didn't mean. I love you.

One thing I do want to say though, which was one reason besides my privileges being taken away that I got mad, was because I can never tell when you're going to lay down the law. This entire week, except for Tuesday, I left late and yet nothing was said about it. But then today I leave late and get grounded for a week. That got me mad. Because since I was not being grounded all the other times I began to take it easier and easier on myself. But then today you decided to lay down the law when nothing had been done before.

I slept later this morning because last night I studied really late for my midterm. This isn't being said to get me off the hook. But rather it's being written because I'm asking you to be a little more consistent in your discipline so I'll know what to expect and when to expect it.

If you would have laid down the law earlier this week I would have almost served my time. I know I have no right to tell you how to run the family. It's just a suggestion and something to think about. I'm sorry. I really am.

I love you and always will.

David

I thanked him for what he'd written and told him I could see his reasoning. I apologized for threatening to discipline him and waiting far too long before actually doing it. I reaffirmed my love for him too. But I told him he would have to suffer the consequence of his tardiness. After praying with him and coming to an honest understanding, he did some chores, we played some Big Boggle with his mom, we watched some television together, and he just stayed home. Of course, we all went to church on Sunday as the family always does. From that time on he got up fifteen minutes earlier each morning and never had that kind of problem again.

Creative Discipline

Discipline needs to be consistent but not routine. It works best when it is creative. For example, Arlyne wrote down many marvelous consequences on a stack of three-by-five cards. They were placed in a bag. So when the kid did something that required discipline, they would have to draw one of the cards from the bag. Then they would do whatever the card directed. Among the consequences were: "Wash the dishes for a week"; "Pull weeds for two hours"; "Give the dog a bath"; "Read an approved book for two hours"; "Mow the lawn every Saturday for a month"; "Write letters to both sets of grandparents"; "Wash both family cars each week this month"; "Memorize the five Bible verses listed on this card." There were many more.

A paper bag was also placed in our hall closet where Arlyne or I would collect the kids' things left lying around the house. They had to redeem their items by drawing a card from the other bag.

Remember: We raised a bunch of teenagers from broken homes. They loved the three-by-five cards and the bags in the hall closet because it often meant one of them got out of having to do their chore because the one being disciplined had to do it instead!

Stepchildren or Foster Children

Spanking a foster child is against the law and should be. Foster children, or those who come from homes where they were emotionally and physically abused, do not interpret a spanking as an expression of love from anyone. Most of all they will resent or be terrified by a spanking from a stranger or stepparent they haven't fully accepted.

A divorced person who has custody of a child for only part of the time is disadvantaged by spanking the child if the other spouse doesn't. After all, if you were the kid being spanked at one house but not the other, which house would you prefer? The answer is obvious!

If at all possible, divorced parents need to work together to establish the rules for discipline of their children. Consistency in this area will restore a sense of stability and security to their kids.

Otherwise, the paper bag and other creative forms of discipline will probably work far better.

Very Creative Discipline

Lane Arndt, former seminar coordinator for Marriage Plus, and his wife, Andrea, have a beautiful eight-year-old daughter named Kirsten. One day Kirsten fell off her bicycle and broke her arm. While sitting in the emergency ward waiting for the doctor to finish up, she proudly announced, "I guess I won't have to take out the trash anymore."

Lane quickly informed her, "That's fine, Kirsten. But we are going to handle your decision like our government does. You'll have to fill out five pages of forms in order to go on disability. In six weeks you will receive your first check for 20 percent of your allowance!"

Kirsten immediately responded, "I'll keep taking out the trash!"

Reckless Driving Discipline

Edna Quinn of Tampa, Florida, shared this:

My father was an automobile dealer. For my sixteenth birthday he brought home the most beautiful green convertible I'd ever seen. On Saturdays my friends and I would fill several cars and head out to horseback ride. Before long we were racing each other in our cars down private country roads. Then a farmer caught us and vowed to tell our parents.

I shuddered at the thought of my father's anger and his booming voice. But instead he smiled sadly, took my hand and said softly, "I'm sorry. I have an apology to make. I used poor judgment in giving you an automobile. You're so mature in many ways that I thought you were ready for it. You're not. The car will be sold. Please forgive your dad's mistake."

It was difficult to give up that car, but harder to see the disappointment on my father's face. He helped me realize I must be responsible.

Parents: Train Your Children

One reason parents do not discipline their children is because they know they aren't taking the needed time to teach right from wrong. It takes time. There are some vital steps you need to take to establish an environment of discipline in your home.

1. Make a list of rules for each individual child in your home.

2. Take time to explain the rules to each child.

3. Make certain each child understands the rules he is to live by.

4. Make certain each child understands the consequences for breaking the rules.

Each family will need to consider its own particular situation. You may add two or three more rules that apply to your own family. But these following rules are absolutes that need to be included:

1. Absolute obedience. Clearly tell your child to do something once, and if they don't obey, discipline them.

2. Absolute honesty. Your children should never lie to anyone — especially Mom and Dad. If there is such a thing as *the worst sin,* it would have to be the sin of lying. Satan is "the father of lies" (John 8:44). Lying is equal to murder in the mind of God (Rev.

21:8; 22:15) and should receive maximum discipline.

3. Absolutely no sassing. Since both parents represent authority (1 Cor. 11:3), impudence cannot be allowed. It will destroy your authority. Kids may ask honest questions and express their opinions. But rudeness has to be stopped the moment it starts.

4. Absolutely no ridicule; attempting to make a fool of someone; tearing a person down; racial jokes or slurs; constant teasing that hurts someone's feelings; swearing at anyone; or bullying. Never allow name-calling or jokes about anyone's appearance or ability. Any of these types of behavior can cause deep emotional pain and destructive bitterness for a lifetime.

Keep your list of rules long enough to meet the needs in your family but short enough to be remembered. Don't punish children for being children.

How Do You Enforce Rules?

If your children love you, your love and prayers will be your greatest strengths. Live the joy of the Christian life in front of them. Love them and make sure they know you do. But be consistent in keeping the rules. Never support their sin or allow them to sin in your home. Remember the Holy Spirit is your strength (Eph. 6:10), and Christ is working with you as you continue to call on Him (2 Cor. 6:1-2).

Your children can be trained to respect the rules in your home. Kids are born with a God-given need for discipline and direction. It will be much easier to enforce the rules if you have taken the time to develop a positive attitude about discipline.

Train up a child in the way he should go,
Even when he is old he will not depart from it (Prov. 22:6).

Appeal through their sense of humor.

Help your child develop a sense of humor. Don't allow your kids to stay in negative, grumpy moods. If they are acting as though both you and the world are horrible, get them to do a chore or activity, not necessarily as discipline, but to get their minds on something else.

Never let yourself or your kids surrender to dark moods. When anyone does that they are surrendering to the devil. Second Corinthians 10:5 says, "Taking every thought captive." We are to be in charge of our own thought-life (Phil. 4:4-9).

Don't allow whining to be a part of your kids' lives. There is a stage in life when children may develop into whiners. Their voice will suddenly sound as if it was replaced with a moaning siren. Stop it quickly!

Tell them you can't understand them when they whine. Ignore them if they keep whining. But stop everything else you are doing and listen instantly when the whining stops. (Sending them to their room for fifteen minutes can help your nerves at such a time too!)

Honest tears are not whining. Honest tears are OK. In fact, a young girl entering puberty often finds herself breaking into tears at the most unusual times. She probably will be extremely embarrassed about this. Understand and reassure her that emotions are physiologically connected at such times. Boys may have this same kind of experience. There is nothing *unmasculine* about male tears. Jesus wept in John 11:35.

Be certain all children four or under get a nap during the day. A crying, whining child is often an exhausted child. Moms, it is not a bad idea for you to get a nap too. That will often give you the extra energy you need when Dad gets home from work.

Appeal through their conscience.

Teach your kids to do right because God commands it. Teach them to be loving and caring to others. Encourage them to stop and think about the right way to respond in situations and to avoid overreacting.

Teach your children to say "thank you" and "please" when they are very young. It is something they should never stop doing. Teach them the importance of politeness and good manners. Be their example.

Conscience is strong in young people. Recently an elementary school principal was annoyed when he saw two boys whispering rather than listening to a guest speaker during an assembly. Finally he announced, "I expect the two rude boys who have been creating a disturbance to come to my office after school and apologize for their lack of good manners." At the end of the school day, thirty-two boys were lined up in front of the principal's office!

Of course, there are exceptions. Little Oxnard brought home what is now called his "Watergate report card." First he denied there was one. Then he couldn't find it. When he finally located it, three grades had been erased!

Appeal through a sense of pride.

Let's get something straight. *Pride* that means "self-righteousness" can cause anyone to stumble and fall away from the Lord. Hardly anything is more intolerable than a smug, cocky person. God hates that kind of pride (Prov. 8:13).

But there is another kind of pride — the God-honoring kind. It is found in people who recognize nothing good is within them except what Christ put there (1 Cor. 1:31). It also recognizes Christ and His great work in others. It doesn't mind praising others — especially kids — when Christ achieves something in or through another's life (John 17:22-23).

It feels good to feel good. When you let your kids know they've done something wonderful, it will make the whole family feel good. Every child equates his own worth by doing well with the gifts and talents God has given them. So help your kids find things they can achieve in doing.

Amplifying the Truth

In the Amplified Bible, Proverbs 22:6 says, "Train up a child in the way they should go and in keeping with his individual gift or bent."

Watch for the areas where your children show particular ability. Their interests may change. But do whatever you can to encourage these gifts from God. Be certain they and you give that gift proper time to develop.

What to Do With a Real Rebel

Many teenagers today represent a spoiled nation that has majored in permissiveness and denied God. Even kids raised in Christian homes may rebel against the restraints of a disciplined life because they want to be like their unrestrained friends (1 Cor. 15:33).

Any rebels, however, can be set free from their bondages by receiving Jesus Christ as Lord and Savior. Parents uniting with a pastor and church youth group that ministers truth and life through the Word of God, can bring transformation through the power of the Holy Spirit (Phil. 1:6). God, who is big enough to transform rebels such as the apostle Paul, Nicky Cruz or Chuck Colson, is big enough to transform *any* rebel!

James Dobson, in his book *Parenting Isn't for Cowards*, writes:

> Instead of groveling and whining, parents of rebellious teens are encouraged to stand firm and take appropriate action. This may include taking away the family car, restricting use of the telephone and refusing to intervene when the teen is in jail. It may also include locking a drug user out of the home. A note on the front door informs him he will be welcome only if he enrolls in a drug rehab program.[12]

Ministry to a rebel must be a combination of love, training and discipline. If it is not possible to combine these things in the rebel's home, then outside help may be the only answer. There are many outstanding Christian youth ranches and homes for kids who otherwise might end up as throwaway kids.

My favorite youth ranch for kids is KLEOS. Gordon and Vicki Hankins and an excellent staff run this permanent Christian youth ranch twelve months a year near Klamath Falls, Oregon. KLEOS takes in children or teens who are young rebels or kids from homes where parents are having problems of their own. The Hankinses and their coworkers train and carefully disciple these kids to be responsible citizens. After staying as long as needed, the kids often return in wholeness to their own parents. For full information write to KLEOS, P.O. Box 141, Klamath Falls, OR 97601; (503) 783-2220.

Rebels Speak to Parents

Ann Landers has several times published a list of ten rules for parents written by a group of young lawbreakers in a correctional institute. Here are some of the things these rebels wanted to say to all parents:

242

1. Keep cool. Don't lose your temper in the crunch. Kids need the reassurance that comes from controlled responses.

2. Don't get strung out from too much booze or too many pills. Remember: Your children are great imitators. We lose respect for parents who tell us to behave one way, while they are behaving another way.

3. Bug us a little. Be strict and consistent in dishing out discipline. Show us who's boss. It gives us a feeling of security to know we've got some strong support under us.

4. Don't blow your class. Keep the dignity of parenthood. Stay on that pedestal. Your children have put you there because they need somebody to look up to. Don't try to dress, dance or talk like your kids. You embarrass us and you look ridiculous.

5. Light a candle. Show us the way. Tell us God is not dead, sleeping or on vacation. We need to believe in something bigger and stronger than ourselves.

6. If you catch us lying, stealing or being cruel, get tough. Let us know why what we did was wrong. Impress on us the importance of not repeating such behavior. When we need discipline, dish it out. But let us know you still love us, even though we have let you down.

7. Call our bluff. Make it clear you mean what you say. Don't be wishy-washy. Don't compromise. And don't be intimidated by our threats to drop out of school or leave home. Stand firm. If you collapse, we will know we beat you down, and we will not be happy about the victory. Kids don't want everything they ask for.

8. Be honest with us. Tell the truth no matter what. And be straight-arrow about it. Lukewarm answers make us uneasy. We can smell uncertainty a mile away. This means being generous with praise. If you give us kids a few compliments once in a while, we will be able to accept criticism more readily. We want you to tell it like is.[13]

It's Up to You

God calls on fathers to raise their kids in the love and discipline of the Lord (Eph. 6:4). Mothers are to do this too (Eph. 6:1). Cruelty warps even formerly healthy minds. But when God's love, discipline and definite boundaries are used in a home, the family will rejoice forever over the results.

Parents who are afraid to put their foot down usually have kids who step on their toes!

Dear Ray:

Our only son marries this Saturday. We have been very close. He's been a Christian since childhood, but he's marrying a relatively new Christian. We like her but just aren't sure she's the best one he could have chosen. We don't know what to do. We will, of course, attend the wedding as his parents. But what should we tell him *now*? And how should we act toward them afterward if we object to things they are doing? Could you give us some guidelines for parents whose children have flown the coop?

Praying Hard

For this cause a man shall leave
his father and mother, and cleave
to his wife; and the two shall
become one flesh.
Ephesians 5:31

THIRTEEN

DON'T GRIEVE WHEN THEY LEAVE TO CLEAVE

Marriage counselors tell us a woman usually marries a man who reminds her of her father. That may be the reason why mothers cry at weddings!

TIM WAS TWENTY-TWO years old, and we knew our son well. So the twinkle in his eye and grin on his face were a real tip-off. He and Kelly Nelson, his girlfriend for more than two years, had a big announcement to make and could hardly wait to make it. His tight grip on her hand gave us the clue that his announcement had to do with her.

Suddenly Tim said: "Dad and Mom, Kelly and I are in love. We think God has brought us together, and we want to get married next year. We've come to ask for your blessing. And we want you to tell us if you see anything in either of us that you think would keep us from having a great marriage."

Arlyne and I were thrilled for both of them. We knew they'd be a great match, and they *are*. Kelly's parents, Jim and Diane Nelson, are both staff members at Church on the Way. They have a marvelous marriage, and their example has given Kelly a strong foundation. Tim treasures the relationship he has with them. Wonderful in-laws are like having a lot of money in the bank. It feels good and provides a great sense of security. Tim and Kelly went to her parents and received their blessings too.

Tim and Kelly's asking us for our blessing on their marriage was not *old-fashioned* or *quaint* — it was biblical.

The directions are very clear for a married couple: "leave to cleave." Without leaving Mama's apron strings or Dad's financial control (or vice versa), the marriage won't work well. Marriage is for mature Christians (Matt. 7:24-27; 2 Cor. 6:14-15). That's why the world does such a bad job at marriage.

> Unless the Lord builds the house,
> They labor in vain who build it (Ps. 127:1).

Giving the Bride Away

At times someone will point out that Ephesians 5:31 tells the *man* to leave his parents but doesn't tell the *woman* to leave hers. The people to whom Paul was speaking lived in the first century. They would have thought it strange if Paul gave any such instruction for women. Every follower of God in that day knew the bride *always* left her parents' covering for her husband's covering. One of the major phrases used for marriage at that time was to *take* a wife (Gen. 24:4; 28:6; Matt. 1:20).

Even to this day fathers traditionally "give away their daughters" at the altar. But this is far more than a tradition in God's eyes. It is precisely at this point — at the wedding — that a father in reality is to *give his daughter away* to her groom. That act will put into motion God's directions for the newly married couple:

> But I want you to understand that Christ is the head of every man, and the man is the head of a woman, and God is the head of Christ (1 Cor. 11:3).

When this verse is placed alongside Ephesians 5:22-25, its meaning becomes clearer.

> Wives, be subject to your own husbands, as to the Lord. For the husband is the head of the wife, as Christ also is the head of the church, He Himself being the Savior of the body. But as the church is subject to Christ, so also the wives ought to be to their husbands in everything. Husbands, love your wives, just as Christ also loved the church and gave Himself up for her (Eph. 5:22-25).

No one is to come between the Lord and you. Nor is a parent, or anyone else, ever to come between a married son or daughter and his or her spouse. The parent's spiritual authority by word, or any other method except personal prayer, is removed by the Lord when the son or daughter marries. A spirit of control in a parent over his or her married child, or a discouraging word about the child's husband or wife, is sin. It totally violates the Word of God.

When Tim and Kelly became engaged, they had one year to continue dating as singles before their marriage. Only during that year would Arlyne and I, or Jim and Diane, be allowed by God to "speak into" our son or daughter's life with the spiritual authority God had given us at their births.

Before their wedding we still had a God-given "authority" (1 Cor. 11:3) to point out any problems we felt they might encounter if they married. By doing so, it would give them the opportunity to overcome such problems during their year of dating. But once they were pronounced man and wife, the spiritual authority *instantly* and *completely* passed from parent to husband. (Read my book *Marriage Plus* for an in-depth discussion of spiritual authority).

Grandparenting

Tim and Kelly's children, Brennon and Kaelyn Mossholder (our first grandchildren), are a sheer joy to us. At three and a half, Brennon can throw a ball straight as an arrow. And one-year-old Kaelyn's smile would charm the flowers off the wallpaper. Want to see more snapshots?!

Tragically, many grandparents don't get the blessing of regularly being with their grandchildren. Generally, this is the result of our mobile society and broken families. Grandparents, even from a distance, need to keep a close relationship. This requires creativity. Postcards, telephones and fax machines can be part of the answer. So can audio cassette tapes with your message or stories you read aloud to your grandchildren. Nothing, of course, takes the place of wonderful visits and vacations together. The bond needs to remain intact.

The goal of grandparenting remains the same wherever you live — to keep on cheering for the home team. We had no right then and have no right now, unless we are specifically asked by Tim or Kelly, to advise them about what to do or not to do in their marriage or their parenting. God has commanded Tim to "cherish his wife" and "give himself up" (Eph. 5:25). He is to lead his family lovingly (Eph. 5:23) with Kelly's insight, input and cooperation. Tim is coach (1 Cor. 11:3), and Kelly is his star quarterback. Arlyne and I are on their team to give godly answers to their direct verbal questions only if they ask for our advice. Otherwise we just sit in the bleachers, wave our pom-poms, cheer for them and pray!

Oh, and along with Kelly's folks, we make the best free baby-sitters their children could ever have — and we love it!

Sometimes Grandparents Have to Take Back the Authority

Only a severe spiritual violation by a son or daughter's spouse (adultery, spouse beating, incest, drug addiction or alcoholism) would ever create such destruction to their wedding covenant that, in order to protect the non-covenant breaker and their children, a parent would need to step into the situation once again with Christ's authority. If that happens, it would be necessary to: 1) put the victims in a protected, safe place (this may be the parent's home); and 2) reach out in love to the covenant-breaker, seeking to get proper Christian counsel for them in order that hopefully they might soon be restored to Christ and their marriage (Gal. 6:1-2).

There are fifty-four million grandparents in America today. One in three adults is a grandparent. Approximately 5 percent of grandparents begin a brand-new family with their own grandchildren. Death, divorce or tragic circumstances make this necessary. If, for whatever reason, both a grandchild's mother and father are financially, physically or spiritually unable to care for their children, the grandparents can be given full authority under 1 Corinthians 11:3 to raise the children until that situation changes and the kids can be safely restored to their parents. During this time a grandparent has to concentrate on loving and raising the kids, not on mentally injuring them with verbal attacks against their struggling or fallen parent(s).

Moving Away

David kissed us good-bye, left on an airplane for Tulsa, Oklahoma, and is sorely missed by his mom and me. In the past three and a half years, we've been together for Christmas and a few weeks during the summers. Although he is not married and we have always had a great relationship, David is still too far away from home for us to be his constant spiritual authorities. Who provides a spiritual covering for him until he marries or returns home to us?

> Obey your leaders, and submit to them; for they keep watch over your souls, as those who will give an account. Let them do this with joy and not with grief, for this would be unprofitable for you (Heb. 13:17).

In David's case it is the godly leaders at Oral Roberts University who have the spiritual authority over his life. David has been chaplain of his wing at ORU for two years and is a resident advisor in his dorm this year. But he has a Christ-centered campus chaplain and pastor to counsel him.

Ma Bell once again is a friend in need whenever David desires parental counsel. Because we've been close all his life, and he's comfortable in our love, he (like all of our kids) doesn't hesitate to ask for our counsel.

Those singles who are not in a Christ-centered college or university but are away from home should be in a great church where they will find the same kind of authority and spiritual counsel available to them through pastors and counselors.

How can you know if a church or individual is the right kind of spiritual authority?

Any qualified counseling authority must live an honest, Christian lifestyle, one which your son or daughter would want to imitate (1 Cor. 11:1). This should also be true for the pastors and elders at the church where you and your family are attending now.

> Remember those who led you, who spoke the word of God to you; and considering the outcome of their way of life, imitate their faith (Heb. 13:7).

If your Christian son or daughter wouldn't want to be like the leaders of the church they are attending, they should change churches. The same is true for you.

The Lantern Carrier

The bearded young man sat across from me for the very first time. We were having lunch together at a Baltimore restaurant. At a certain moment he leaned across the table and said, "Sir, I am sure I am in love with your daughter. What could I do to win her as my wife?"

I told him, "I'm not sure you ever could. Elizabeth loves the Lord with all her heart. But if God is in this, all I can tell you is to cram as much of the Bible in you as you can and live the Christian life. Then there is a slight chance you could win her!"

Todd Hinson continued to do exactly what I told him. Already a sincere Christian, he followed Christ right into Elizabeth's heart. And there they were two years later at their wedding, with Elizabeth carrying a lit lantern down the aisle.

Today Todd is the administrator of the Marriage Plus ministry. In that role I can speak to him as his boss. But I have no right to control his and Beth's marriage. Thank God that they have a beautiful one.

As this book was being written, Elizabeth and Todd announced that she is pregnant. Look out, world — here comes another great kid!

And So the World Continues

Larry Jack, Diane Griffith, Katy Tozier and several others of the kids Arlyne and I helped raise as teenagers have wonderful marriages. Most have strong and restored relationships with their own parents too. In fact, Larry spoke recently at the funeral of his

Christian uncle, and fifteen of his relatives gave their lives to Christ.

That's the goal — to bring restoration and wholeness to families. Any nation with strong and united families will be a great nation.

It is impossible to know what God will do in the immediate future. There is a constant spiritual battle being waged for our families now that will decide this nation's fate. As Ephesians 6:12 clearly tells us:

> For our struggle is not against flesh and blood, but against the rulers, against the powers, against the world forces of this darkness, against the spiritual forces of wickedness in the heavenly places.

No nation can murder more than thirty-one million babies and not be judged by God. The only hope for America is a genuine spiritual and moral revival. It must begin with you. This is no time to retreat, but a time to advance and raise or restore our families in Christ. Pray and work, too, for godly governmental leadership that will create and restore righteous laws in America.

> If my people, who are called by my name, shall humble themselves, and pray, and seek my face, and turn from their wicked ways; then will I hear from heaven, and will forgive their sin, and will heal their land (2 Chron. 7:14, KJV).

We cannot have a change in circumstances unless we have a change in character.

NOTES

Chapter One
Kids *Are* a Plus

1. American Demographics Desk Reference, July 1992, p. 8.

2. "Current Population Report: Marital Status and Living Arrangements," Report P20-478, March 1993, p. 1, U.S. Bureau of the Census.

3. "Household and Family Characteristics," Report P20-477, p. 1, U.S. Bureau of the Census.

4. Louis S. Richman, "Struggling to Save Our Kids," *Fortune,* Aug. 10, 1992, p. 35.

5. Myron Magnet, "The American Family 1992," *Fortune,* Aug. 10, 1992, pp. 43-44.

6. Ibid.

7. "Marital Status and Living Arrangements," 1994, U.S. Bureau of the Census.

8. Margaret L. Usdansky, "More Kids Live in Changing Family," *USA Today,* August 30, 1994, p. A1.

9. "Advance Report of Final Natality Statistics," 1991, published in 1993, National Center for Health Statistics; Vital Statistics of the United States.

10. Statistical information from the U.S. Census Bureau; endangered species information from a list of the top one hundred endangered species in *Life* magazine, September 1994, pp. 53, 58.

11. Donald J. Hernandez, *America's Children: Resources From Family, Government, and the Economy,* 1993 (Population of the United States in the 1980s: A Census Monograph Series), Russell Sage, publisher, U.S. Bureau of the Census.

12. "Marital Status and Living Arrangements," Report P20-478, March 1993, p. xi, U.S. Bureau of the Census.

13. Margaret L. Usdansky, "More Kids Live in Changing Family," *USA Today,* August 30, 1994, p. A1.

14. Louis S. Richman, "Struggling to Save Our Kids," *Fortune,* Aug. 10, 1992, p. 35.

15. Marilyn Elias, "One in Four Kids Suffers Some Form of Abuse," *USA Today,* Oct. 3, 1994, p. D1.

16. Ad in *USA Today* by The New American Revolution, Oct. 13, 1994, p. 9B.

17. James Dobson, *The Strong-Willed Child* (Wheaton, Ill.: Tyndale House Publishers Inc., 1978), p. 20.
18. Douglas Copeland, *Life After God* (New York: Pocket Books, division of Simon & Schuster, 1994), p. 181.
19. Letters, *U.S. News & World Report,* May 16, 1994, p. 6.

Chapter Two
God Wants to Save Your Whole Family

1. Isabel Wilkerson, "The Most Dangerous Criminals in America Are Also the Youngest," *The New York Times,* May 16, 1994, p. 1. Copyright © 1994 by The New York Times Company. Reprinted by permission.
2. Ibid.

Chapter Three
The World Has Fallen, and It Can't Get Up

1. "In Quotes," *USA Today,* April 1, 1994, p. 13A.
2. Robert James Bidinotto, "Must Our Prisons Be Resorts?" *Readers' Digest,* November 1994, pp. 69-70.
3. From *Meinkampf,* Vol. 1, 1933, as quoted in *Familiar Quotations* by John Bartlett, edited by Emily Morison Beck (Boston: Little, Brown and Company, 1980), p. 812.
4. *Time,* "How Man Began" by Michael D. Lemonick, March 14, 1994, p. 81.
5. Dennis Petersen, *Unlocking the Mysteries of Creation,* Vol. 1 (El Dorado, CA.: Creation Resource Foundation, p. 63.
6. Rex Beasley, *Edison* (Philadelphia: Chilton Company, 1964), p. 95.
7. Nathan McCall, "My Rap Against Rap," *Washington Post,* Nov. 14, 1993, pp. C1, C4.
8. John Dewey, *The Early Works of John Dewey, Early Essays 1882-1898* (London and Amsterdam: Southern Illinois University Press, Feffer and Simons Inc., 1972), p. 54. Dewey argued against a need for any form of organized religion, including Christianity. He did so because he saw religion as a method that sought to make all humans conform to a certain set of absolutes. In Dewey's mind religion isolated only certain individuals, but the entire nation could be taught his form of humanism, "freeing" humans never to feel guilty, since all were required to attend school in their formative years.

9. Aldous Huxley, *Ends and Means, an Inquiry Into the Nature of Ideals, and Into the Methods Employed for Their Realization* (New York and London: Harper and Brothers, 1937), pp. 312, 315, 316.

Chapter Four
Our "Dangerous" Holy Bible

1. Alex Ayres, ed., *The Wit and Wisdom of Mark Twain* (New York: Meridian Penguin Books, 1987).
2. Patrick J. Buchanan, "Leftist Bashing of Christians Is All the Rage," *Los Angeles Daily News,* June 15, 1994, p. 15.
3. David Barton, *America: To Pray or Not to Pray* (Aledo, Tex.: WallBuilder Press, 1991), p. 19.
4. Ibid., p. 53.
5. Taken from a commencement address delivered by Ted Koppel to the 1987 graduating class of Duke University on May 10, 1987.
6. *Stone V. Gramm,* 449 U.S. 39,42, 1980.
7. *Jager v. Douglas,* 862F. 2d 824, 825; 11th Cir.
8. *Roberts v. Madigan,* 702 F. Supp. 1505, 1507; Denver, Colorado.
9. Frank S. Mead, ed., *12,000 Religious Quotations* (Grand Rapids, Mich.: Baker Book House, 1989), p. 189.
10. Ibid., p. 23.
11. Ibid., p. 28.
12. Noah Webster, *The History of the United States* (New Haven, Conn.: Durrie & Peck, 1833), p. 309.
13. Frank S. Mead, ed., *12,000 Religious Quotations* (Grand Rapids, Mich.: Baker Book House, 1989), p. 29.
14. Larry Burkett, *Whatever Happened to the American Dream* (Chicago: Moody Press, 1993), p. 71.
15. Frank S. Mead, *12,000 Religious Quotations* (Grand Rapids, Mich.: Baker Book House, 1989), p. 30.
16. James Madison, *Notes of Debates in the Federal Convention of 1787* (New York: W.W. Norton & Co., original: 1787, reprinted 1987), pp. 209-210.
17. Burkett, *Whatever Happened to the American Dream?,* p. 72.
18. "Sexually Transmitted Disease Surveillance 1992," U.S. Dept. of Health & Human Services, Centers for Disease Control and Prevention.
19. *Criminal Victimization in the United States,* U.S. Bureau of Justice Statistics, pp. 195-196.
20. Ibid., pp. 196, 198.
21. Ibid., p. 94.

22. William Linn, *The Life of Jefferson* (Ithaca, N.Y.: Mack and Andrus, 1834), p. 265.

23. "Spirit of the South Bay," Jubilee Christian Center, 175 Nortech Parkway, San Jose, CA 95134.

24. William Murray, "America Without God," *The New American,* June 20, 1988, p. 19.

25. David Barton, *The Myth of Separation: What Is the Correct Relationship Between Church and State? — A Revealing Look at What the Founders and Early Courts Really Said* (Aledo, Tex.: WallBuilder Press).

26. Tony Mauro, "Many students don't want to graduate without a prayer," *USA Today,* June 3, 1994, p. 3A.

Chapter Seven
Bonding, and I Don't Mean James

1. Guy Doud, "With Love to Hurting Teens," Focus on the Family broadcast, September 27, 1993.

2. Dr. Urie Broffenbrenner, "Where's Dad?," Focus on the Family broadcast, September 24-26, 1993.

Chapter Nine
Your Word Is Your Bond

1. Hermine Hartley, *The Family Book of Manners* (Uhrichsville, Oh.: Barbour & Co., 1990).

2. Foster Cline and Jim Fay, *Parenting With Love and Logic: Teaching Children Responsibility* (Colorado Springs, Colo.: Navpress, 1990), pp. 133-135.

Chapter Ten
How Essential Is School?

1. "The Endangered Summer Vacation," *U.S. News & World Report,* May 16, 1994, p. 12.

2. Jeffrey Burke Satinover, M.D., "Outcome Based Education Analysis," Committee to Save Our Schools (CTSOS), Westport, Connecticut.

3. *The Phyllis Schlafly Report,* Vol. 26, No. 10, May 1993.

4. Survey conducted by Christian Equippers International, 2100 Eloise Ave., South Lake Tahoe, CA; 1-800-662-0909.

5. Ibid.
6. Ibid.
7. Louis Uchitelle, "Wages of College-educated Men Slip Despite Economic Growth," *Los Angeles Daily News*, September 5, 1994, p. 16.
8. *Great Book of Funny Quotes: Witty Words for Every Day of the Year,* (New York: Sterling Publishing Co. Inc., 1993), p. 36.
9. Kim Painter, "Safe-sex Solution: Condoms in Dorms," *USA Today,* September 19, 1987.

Chapter Eleven
When Are They Ready to Date?

1. "Sexual Activity Among American Teens," U.S. Dept. of Human Services/Public Health Service Statistics, Vol. 116, *Washington Post,* July 20, 1993, p. 5.

2. *Sex and America's Teenagers,* The Alan Guttmacher Institute, New York and Washington, 1994, p. 19.

3. Paula M. Braverman and Victor C. Strasburger, "Adolescent Sexual Activity; Adolescent Sexuality Part One," *Clinical Pediatrics*, November 1993, p. 658.

4. Division of STD/HIV Prevention Annual Report: 1992, U.S. Dept. of Health & Human Services, Public Health Service, Centers for Disease Control and Prevention, National Center for Prevention Services, p. 29.

5. Joseph P. Shapiro, "The Teen Pregnancy Boom," *U.S. News & World Report,* July 13, 1992, p. 38.

6. *Society: Social Costs of Teenage Sexuality,* Social Science and the Citizen, Vol. 30, September-October 1993, p. 3.

7. *USA Today* quoting *Sex and America's Teenagers,* a report by the Alan Guttmacher Institute, June 7, 1994, p. 6-D.

8. Ibid.
9. Ibid.
10. Ibid.
11. Ibid.
12. Ibid.
13. Bill Uselton, "Sex Education for Two-Year-Olds," *Bible in the News,* distributed by The Gospel Truth, Southwest Radio Church of the Air, Oklahoma City, Oklahoma, March/April 1994.

14. *Sex and America's Teenagers,* a report published by The Alan Guttmacher Institute, New York, 1994, pp. 38, 41.

15. Traditional Values Coalition, 100 S. Anaheim Blvd., Ste. 350, Anaheim, CA 92805.

16. Josh McDowell, *Why Wait?*, Nashville, Tenn.: Thomas Nelson, 1987.

17. Ibid.

Chapter Twelve
Kids Need to Know the Rules

1. Isabel Wilkerson, "The Most Dangerous Criminals in America Are Also Its Youngest," *The News Tribune*, Tacoma, Washington, p. 1.

2. Roland Kotulak, *Chicago Tribune*.

3. "Attempted Suicide Among High School Students — United States, 1990," *Morbidity and Mortality Weekly Report*, September 20, 1991, p. 633.

4. "Deaths of Teenagers From Firearms Reach Historic High," v108 Public Health Reports, July-August 1993, p. 517.

5. "A Drug Problem Oft Overlooked — Alcohol Abuse by Teenagers," *Tufts University Diet and Nutrition Letter*, January 1992, p. 6.

6. "Alcohol Remains the 'Drug of Choice' in High School — 8th Grade Use Climbs," *The Alcoholism Report*, April 1993, p. 8.

7. "Two Youth Surveys Released; Alcohol Remains Drug of Choice," *The Alcoholism Report* (20th Anniversary Edition), v. 20, p. 2.

8. "Teen Drug Use, Attitudes Worsen," v. 6, *Alcoholism and Drug Abuse Weekly*, February 7, 1994, p. 2.

9. Tom Alexander, Teen Scene, Box 10551, Bakersfield, CA 93389, (805) 324-TEEN.

10. Statistics in this section were taken from the following sources: *Ladies' Home Journal*, January 1986; *Newsweek*, April 25, 1988; *Parents'* Magazine, January 1988; *Psychology Today*, January 1988; *Seventeen*, March 1989.

11. Laura Myers, "Homeless Teenagers Envision No Future," *San Mateo* (California) *Times*, November 1992, local section.

12. James C. Dobson, *Parenting Isn't for Cowards* (Dallas: Word Publishing, 1987), p. 170.

13. Ann Landers, *Los Angeles Valley Daily News,* April 15, 1979. Permission granted by Ann Landers/Creators Syndicate.

I'd like very much to know what this book
means to you. Please write or call.

I've narrated audio cassettes for this book,
Kids Are *a Plus*, with questions at the end of each chapter.
Also available is a two-tape series, "Real Family Values"
and "Raising Children and Teenagers,"
that I use as part of my Marriage Plus seminar.
Other tapes are available, as well as my books
Marriage Plus and *Singles Plus*.

For information about scheduling or attending any
of our seminars or for a catalog of audio and video tapes
of *Marriage Plus* or *Singles Plus* and other messages
by Ray and Arlyne Mossholder, write or call:

Marriage Plus
P.O. Box 45100
Tacoma, WA 98374-0100
206-848-6400

If you enjoyed *Kids* Are *a Plus*, you'll love these
other Creation House titles:

Marriage Plus
by Ray Mossholder
Ray Mossholder uses the Bible and real-life examples to show
what a rich and rewarding relationship God intended marriage
to be. He helps you discover the principles that will allow you to
experience this fullness in your marriage.

Singles Plus
by Ray Mossholder
With the same straightforward approach he brought to Marriage
Plus, Mossholder tackles the issues facing Christian singles. His
probe into the single life offers biblical insight on such topics as
dating, real love versus infatuation, being single the second time
around and the wrong reasons for getting married.

Available at your local Christian bookstore or from:

Creation House
600 Rinehart Road
Lake Mary, FL 32746
1-800-283-8494